THE STRANGE CAREER OF LEGAL LIBERALISM

THE STRANGE CAREER
OF LEGAL LIBERALISM

LAURA KALMAN

YALE UNIVERSITY PRESS   NEW HAVEN AND LONDON

IN MEMORY OF MELANIE MANN BRONFMAN

AND WESTLAKE SCHOOL

PUBLISHED WITH ASSISTANCE FROM THE MARY CADY TEW MEMORIAL FUND.

DESIGNED BY SONIA L. SCANLON
SET IN SABON WITH COPPERPLATE DISPLAY TYPE BY RAINSFORD
TYPE, DANBURY, CONNECTICUT.
PRINTED IN THE UNITED STATES OF AMERICA BY
BOOKCRAFTERS, INC., CHELSEA, MICHIGAN.

LIBRARY OF CONGRESS CATALOGING-IN-PUBLICATION DATA
KALMAN, LAURA, 1955–
THE STRANGE CAREER OF LEGAL LIBERALISM / LAURA KALMAN.
P. CM.
INCLUDES BIBLIOGRAPHICAL REFERENCES AND INDEX.
ISBN 0-300-06369-5 (ALK. PAPER)
1. UNITED STATES—CONSTITUTIONAL LAW—PHILOSOPHY.
2. UNITED STATES—CONSTITUTIONAL LAW—INTERPRETATION AND
CONSTRUCTION. 3. LIBERALISM—UNITED STATES—HISTORY—20TH
CENTURY. 4. LAW—UNITED STATES—METHODOLOGY—
HISTORY. I. TITLE.
KF4552.K35 1996
342.73'001—DC20
[347.30201] 95-47297
CIP

A CATALOGUE RECORD FOR THIS BOOK IS AVAILABLE FROM THE BRITISH LIBRARY.

THE PAPER IN THIS BOOK MEETS THE GUIDELINES FOR PERMANENCE
AND DURABILITY OF THE COMMITTEE ON PRODUCTION GUIDELINES
FOR BOOK LONGEVITY OF THE COUNCIL ON LIBRARY RESOURCES.

10 9 8 7 6 5 4 3 2 1

CONTENTS

ACKNOWLEDGMENTS

Many people have helped me with this book, though none should be blamed for its errors or polemics. I thank Joyce Appleby, Robert Gordon, Hendrik Hartog, Linda Kerber, Martha Minow, and Avi Soifer for commenting on portions of it. I am grateful to Gregory Alexander, Bernard Bailyn, J. M. Balkin, John Blum, Rena Fraden, Jon Glickstein, Morton Horwitz, Sanford Levinson, Frank Michelman, William E. Nelson, David M. Rabban, Jack Rakove, John Reid, John Henry Schlegel, Mark Tushnet, G. Edward White, Joan Williams, and Rosemarie Zagarri for reading the entire manuscript and making many helpful suggestions. I am also obliged to colleagues and friends: Ahkil Amar, Patricia Bagley, Mia Bay, W. Elliot Brownlee, Wallace Chafe, Bill Felstiner, Hope Firestone, Jamie Gracer, Susan Hunt, Leslie Jacobs, the late Robert Kelley, W. Davies King, Alan Liu, David Marshall, Ken McCann, Sears McGee, Marianne Mithun, Harry Scheiber, John Schweizer, Judy Shanks, Cybelle Shattuck, Linny Kammer Smith, Ray Solomon, Clyde Spillenger, Meg Taradash, and Candace Waid. Then there is my family: Celeste

Garr, Lee Kalman, and Newton Kalman. Most of all, I thank W. Randall Garr.

I benefited from opportunities to present this work at the law schools of Harvard University, the University of Texas, and the University of Wisconsin; at the history department of Harvard University; and at Harvard's Charles Warren Center for Studies in American History. I greatly appreciate the financial support provided by the University of California, Santa Barbara, Interdisciplinary Humanities Center, and especially the Warren Center.

I thank my manuscript editor, Ruth Veleta, and, at Yale University Press, I thank Otto Bohlman, Charles Grench, Mary Pasti, and especially Cynthia Wells.

Next to working with John Blum, I most enjoyed learning at Westlake School. Smart, funny, and kind, Melanie Mann Bronfman personified what I remember about the school at its best. To her memory and that of Westlake I dedicate this book.

FAITH OF OUR FATHERS

Faith of our fathers! Living still
In spite of dungeon, fire, and sword:
O how our hearts beat high with joy,
Whene'r we hear that glorious word:
Faith of our fathers, holy faith!
We will be true to thee till death.
Episcopalian Hymnal, no. 558 (1982)

This book grew out of my insomnia. For years I staved off wakefulness by reading law reviews. One article in the middle of the night seemed the best soporific. Law review articles no longer serve my purpose: they have become too interesting.

Why? Law professors, who have long ignored the work of historians as important as Charles Beard and Richard Hofstadter, now seem fascinated by them. The debate between Gordon Wood and J. G. A. Pocock is refought in the law reviews. Even more important, legal scholars have enlisted history, as they have drafted other disciplines, in their battle on behalf of legal liberalism.

I use the term *legal liberalism* to refer to trust in the potential of courts, particularly the Supreme Court, to bring about "those specific social reforms that affect large groups of people such as blacks, or workers, or women, or partisans of a particular persuasion; in other words, *policy change with nationwide impact*." Because of the nation's experience with the Warren Court, legal liberalism has been linked to political liberalism since midcentury.[1] The Warren Court established its reputation as liberal bastion in 1954, when it declared school segregation unconstitutional in *Brown* v. *Board of Education*. "I suppose that realistically the reason this case is here was that action couldn't be obtained from Congress," Justice Jackson observed during oral argument of *Brown*. "[W]e must always remember that it was the Court, not Congress or the President, that put an end to official segregation in this country," one federal appellate judge stressed forty years later. "It was the Court, not any other branch of government that for the first time gave meaning to the phrase 'with liberty and justice for all.' " Or, as one law school dean put it, *Brown* "created a societal commitment, launching a value that was before in every meaningful sense unreal." Those who appreciated it believed that *Brown* placed "the quest for racial justice . . . historically, socially, and politically at the center of the quest for constitutional meaning."[2]

For law professors and other liberals, *Brown* was the "paradigmatic event." *Brown* represented "*the* turning point in terms of people's conception of what the law could do," A. E. Dick Howard emphasized. "Where medieval societies had morality plays, we had *Brown*." To a generation of lawyers, *Brown* served as "a sign that law (and therefore we) could play a part in building a better society." The historian C. Vann Woodward later described the reaction to the *Brown* decision in the South as one of "incredulity . . . the Supreme Court was demanding the impossible." But at the time Woodward thought the Court had made the inconceivable attainable. "A unanimous decision, it has all the moral and legal authority of the Supreme Court behind it, and it is unthinkable that it can be indefinitely evaded," he proclaimed in *The Strange Career of Jim Crow*. As the Court reached other, more difficult decisions over the next fifteen years, liberal law professors' and social reformers' faith in the transformative power of the Warren Court grew even stronger.[3]

In 1991, Professor Owen Fiss provided a classic description of the Warren Court's accomplishments:

In the 1950's, America was not a pretty sight. Blacks were systematically disenfranchised and excluded from juries. State-fostered religious practices, like school prayers, were pervasive. Legislatures were grossly gerrymandered and malapportioned. McCarthyism stifled radical dissent, and the jurisdiction of the censor over matters considered obscene or libelous had no constitutional limits. The heavy hand of the law threatened those who publicly provided information and advice concerning contraceptives, thereby imperiling those most intimate of human relationships. The states virtually had a free hand in the administration of justice. Trials often proceeded without counsel or jury. Convictions were allowed to stand even though they turned on illegally seized evidence or on statements extracted from the accused under coercive circumstances. There were no rules limiting the imposition of the death penalty. These practices victimized the poor and disadvantaged, as did the welfare system, which was administered in an arbitrary and oppressive manner. The capacity of the poor to participate in civic activities was also limited by the imposition of poll taxes, court filing fees, and the like.

These were the challenges that the Warren Court took up and spoke to in a forceful manner. The result was *a program of constitutional reform almost revolutionary in its aspiration and, now and then, in its achievements.* Of course the Court did not act in a political or social vacuum. It drew on broad-based social formations like the civil rights and welfare rights movement. At critical junctures, the Court looked to the executive and legislative branches for support. . . . Yet the truth of the matter is that it was the Warren Court that spurred the great changes to follow, and inspired and protected those who sought to implement them.[4]

The same year Fiss wrote, a political scientist was publishing different conclusions. In his 1991 book *The Hollow Hope: Can Courts Bring about Social Change?* Gerald Rosenberg said: "Growing up in the 1960s in a liberal New York City household, I naturally looked to the Supreme Court, identifying it with important liberal decisions." As Rosenberg matured, however, he came to doubt the ability of courts to "produce liberal social change" that would transform society. In *The Hollow Hope,* he presented data to argue that they "almost never" could. Though little empirical evidence had appeared on the Court's role in fostering social reform before he wrote, some readers found Rosenberg's conclusion unsurprising. According to one academic, it is "rather obvious that asking courts to be the engine of fundamental social change in our complex society makes as little sense as using a word processor to cook dinner, or a hair dryer to spray-paint a house: It is simply not the job the machine was designed to do." Rosenberg has suggested such skeptics accompany him on "some of my law school presentations. That old dead horse of judicial efficacy rears up with a vengeance that is sometimes quite frightening."[5]

Many Americans do continue to see the Court as the great engine of social change. True, on the fortieth anniversary of the first decision in *Brown,* one journalist concluded: "For an earlier generation, the Supreme Court's majestic *Brown* decision illuminated a path to equality through the dismantling of segregation. Today, *Brown*'s beacon has dimmed, and in the gloom lurks the fear that no one knows which road now leads to racial reconciliation." Likewise, in 1995, the fortieth anniversary of *Brown II*—the decision ordering the implementation of school desegregation in the South "with all deliberate speed"—it seems obvious there was no speed whatsoever. At least through the Bork battle, however, Americans retained their obsession with the power of the Supreme Court. Why else would they take the Bork nomination so seriously? And most liberal law professors have continued to make *Brown* their lighthouse. Cass Sunstein has observed that they have remained under "the spell of the Warren Court," their faith in it religious and mystical. Their trust in the power of the Court has helped to make constitutional law "the most prestigious field in the legal academy."[6]

In this book, I do not address the question of whether courts can transform society, an issue that has proven of greater interest to political scientists than academic lawyers. Rather, I focus on how law professors have kept the faith in what has been called "the cult of the Court," defined here as confidence in the ability of courts to change society for what judges believe is the better. Legal scholars have remained members of that cult, despite their changing attitude toward the Supreme Court and their anxiety about judicial activism.[7]

Associated with conservative justices who enacted their personal prejudices into law in cases such as *Lochner* v. *New York* (1905), when they struck down regulatory legislation on the grounds it interfered with the "liberty to contract" that the Fourteenth Amendment's due process clause allegedly granted workers, judicial activism initially seemed the child of substantive due process. That doctrine, it was always emphasized, gave judges unusual power. "For the benefit of laymen, Substantive Due Process is the idea that the Court can hold legislation unconstitutional on the ground that the legislature lacked a rational basis for enacting it," one law professor explained in the *New York Times*. Or, as another said, when the Court did "the substantive due process thing," it substituted its judgment for the legislature's. Although substantive due process faded for a time after the constitutional crisis of the 1930s, which culminated in Roosevelt's 1937 attempt to pack the Supreme Court, judicial activism did not. Once the legal realists had questioned the existence of principled decision making, academic lawyers spent the rest of the twentieth century searching for criteria that would enable them to identify objectivity in judicial decisions. "By objectivity I mean that quality of a rule of law which enables it to be applied to similar situations with similar results regardless of the identity of the judges who apply it," one student of the realists explained. That seemingly simple attribute had come to seem elusive, because both the realists and the constitutional crisis had raised the possibility that all judicial opinions, not just those that favored the rich through invocation of neutral-sounding terms such as "liberty to contract" or "substantive due process," were inherently idiosyncratic.[8]

As they struggled to identify how objective judicial decisions should be reached, liberal law professors faced a new obstacle, the Warren Court. In retrospect, the Warren Court came at a bad time for liberal law professors. Though they revered the Warren Court as much as they had reviled the *Lochner* Court, and though many of their students celebrated Warren Court activism, the mission they had set themselves by the time Earl Warren arrived in Washington forced an older generation of law professors to try to prove the decisions of his Court were based on objective foundations of justice. While *Brown* became the seminal decision for a new generation of legal scholars coming to maturity, the task of their elders, who remembered 1937, became difficult during the Warren years. *Brown* spurred the development of both liberal judicial activism and contemporary constitutional theory. For the legal liberals who loved the Warren Court's results, if not its reasoning, and who dominated the law professorate between the New Deal and the Vietnam War, the Warren Court starkly posed "the counter-majoritarian difficulty," the dilemma of legitimating an appointed judiciary in a democracy.[9]

Even after the Warren Court passed into history in 1969, law professors continued to rely on the Court. Abortion rights, for one example, had no better chance of success in the legislatures than school desegregation. Despite widespread sympathy for pregnant women who had consumed thalidomide or contracted German measles, and who sought abortions because they feared birth defects, the reformers working to legalize therapeutic abortions had been successful in only three states by 1967. Even those victories were largely Pyrrhic because the new reform laws proved restrictive, and hospitals and doctors conservative in implementing them. As David Garrow saw in his history of *Roe* v. *Wade,* "more and more signs began to appear that the passage of reform bills might actually serve to illuminate the inadequacy of therapeutic reform and the preferability of the seemingly far more radical step of repeal." Repeal bills rarely survived the legislative process, although in 1970 legislatures finally repealed abortion laws in Hawaii, New York, and Alaska, and a popular referendum on abortion repeal succeeded in Washington. Consequently, the emphasis shifted from "lobbying for reform to litigating for repeal." By 1969, Garrow found, "federal litigation was where almost all of the activists believed the real breakthroughs would come." The first abortion case was filed in federal court in 1969, and soon over twenty cases were on their way to the Supreme Court. *Roe* v. *Wade,* the 1973 case in which Justice Harry Blackmun struck down every abortion law in the country, declaring that during the first trimester of pregnancy, abortion was a fundamental right, "whether it be founded in the Fourteenth Amendment's concept of personal liberty and restrictions upon state action, as we feel it is, or as the District Court determined, in the Ninth Amendment's reservation of rights to the people," was just one of them.[10]

For a new generation of academic lawyers, and for some of their elders, too, *Roe* became a defining case. Professor Pamela Karlan, a 1984 law school graduate, stressed that "*Roe* v. *Wade* has served as a light-ning rod for modern constitutional law; it is the *Brown* v. *Board of Education* of our generation."[11] The reappearance of substantive due process as a tool of judicial authority in 1973, at a time when liberal legal scholars were struggling to rationalize the Warren Court while guarding against conservative judicial activism, seemed to threaten the legitimacy of the Warren Court. Though they appreciated the legaliza-tion of abortion, many law professors despised the Court's appeal to substantive due process in *Roe* and argued that the Court had dodged its duty to ground the right in the Constitution. In a comment rushed to print in the 1973 *Yale Law Journal,* John Hart Ely, one of the Warren Court's staunchest defenders, attacked *Roe* not because it was "bad con-stitutional law" but because it was "*not* constitutional law and gives almost no sense of an obligation to try to be":

> What is frightening about *Roe* is that this super-protected right is not inferable from the language of the Constitution, the framers' thinking respecting the specific problem in any issue, any general value derivable from the provisions they included, or the nation's governable structure. Nor is it explainable in terms of the unusual political impotence of the group judicially protected vis-à-vis the interest that legislatively prevailed over it. And that, I believe— the predictable early reaction to *Roe* notwithstanding ("more of the same Warren-type activism")—is a charge that can responsi-bly be leveled at no other decision of the past twenty years. At times the inferences the Court has drawn from the values the Con-stitution marks for special protection have been controversial, even shaky, but never before has its sense of an obligation to draw one been so obviously lacking.[12]

At least Ely liked the results in *Roe*. "Were I a legislator," he con-ceded, "I would vote for a statute very much like the one the Court ended up drafting." As the years passed, and the Court became more conservative, law professors from various generations found its results as dissatisfying as its reasoning. While Americans increasingly came to see the Court as arbiter of divisive cultural issues, academic lawyers became more distant from the Court and openly hostile to it. This shift was apparent on the right, where, for example, Stephen Presser lamented that the Supreme Court had "lost its way" and condemned it as "the institution that led us into our present wilderness of the spirit." The negative mood was especially evident left of center, where Yale Law School dean Guido Calabresi (now a federal appellate court judge) used the op-ed page of the *New York Times* to declare in 1991: "I despise the current Supreme Court and find its aggressive, willful, statist behavior disgusting."[13]

Yet Calabresi, Ely, and other legal liberals of all ages operate in a twilight zone where Earl Warren receives artificial life support. A recent law review article began: "Earl Warren is dead. A generation of liberal legal scholars continues, nevertheless, to act as if the man and his Court preside over the present." Meanwhile new political perspectives and insights borrowed from other disciplines have led young law professors to question the future of legal liberalism.[14]

Recently, some liberal law professors have reacted to what they perceive as a crisis of legal liberalism by turning to other disciplines themselves. Some have embraced history. The discovery by liberal legal scholars of an eighteenth-century republicanism they can attribute to the Founders responds to the exaltation by conservatives of "original intent." Ironically, and despite the promise it holds out of a virtuous citizenry pursuing communitarian goals, the republican revival in the hands of some law professors attempts to recapture an improved version of the legal and political liberalism that characterized the law school world of the 1960s.

Who are the republican revivalists? "After almost two hundred years, Thomas Jefferson has been proven right: We are all republicans now," one law professor announced in 1995. In fact, not all law professors subscribe to the republican revival. Law professors differ over the identities of republican revivalists, beyond ascribing to them a political location left of center, as much as they disagree about those of the legal realists. Though I would not classify all on it as republican revivalists, my own list of people whose work has been deeply influenced by the republican revival and whose work has significantly affected the way the legal academy understands the republican revival includes Bruce Ackerman, Ahkil Amar, and Owen Fiss of Yale; Sanford Levinson of Texas;

Frank Michelman of Harvard; Suzanna Sherry of Minnesota; Cass Sunstein of Chicago; at times, Gregory Alexander of Cornell; and two legal historians, Morton Horwitz of Harvard and Mark Tushnet of Georgetown.[15]

The republican revivalists' turn to history holds both promise and peril. Soon after the Court handed down decisions that may signal an effort to return the federal government and the interpretation of the Commerce clause to their contours before the New Deal, Linda Greenhouse wrote that conservatives on the Court who are "[b]lowing the dust off the Constitution that was" hope to turn back the clock. History, one of the weapons used by conservatives, can be turned against them. The reorientation toward history holds peril because when law professors colonize other disciplines, they leave themselves open to being judged by different methodological standards. Liberal legal scholars who "abuse" history undermine their credibility. Though this book is one legal liberal's intellectual history of legal liberalism, it does contain an explicitly normative element. I suggest that historians inside and outside the law schools have something to say to academic lawyers, and that both lawyers and historians would benefit from the interchange. I also argue that historians should recognize that the historic turn represents a sensible strategy for legal liberals and that law professors, who yearn for validation from the rest of the academy, should not curry favor with historians by abandoning the attempt to discern original meanings of the Constitution.[16]

Thus my epigraph is relevant in two respects. The "faith of our fathers" is the trust generations of law professors placed in legal liberalism. Further, just as the hymn "Faith of Our Fathers" was written by nineteenth-century Anglo-Catholics working to erase the Reformation by creating a "Catholic" past for the Church of England, so originalism may prove a useful fiction.[17]

My perspective is that of a scholar educated as both lawyer and historian, who identifies with historians, but whose dual training and career in a history department makes her something of an outsider to both disciplines. My outsider's perspective is reflected in my notation style, in which I have combined the aspects of law professors' and historians' citation practices I like best. Part I provides an intellectual history of legal liberalism. In chapter 1, I examine how legal realism, the constitutional crisis of 1937, and legal and political liberalism affected the way law professors wrote about the Supreme Court from the 1930s until the 1970s. In chapter 2, I show how law professors in the 1970s harnessed other disciplines to their efforts to legitimate legal liberalism. Nevertheless, new political perspectives within the legal academy and demographic changes threatened legal liberalism. As I demonstrate in chapter 3, the threat was not that great. Chapter 4 is a description of how interdisciplinary scholarship challenged both legal liberalism and the search for principled decision making in the early 1980s. The ensuing intellectual and political polarization in the law schools is placed within the context of parallel developments in other disciplines. In chapter 5, I explain how the search for solutions by legal scholars to the crisis of legal liberalism led some of them to history. In Part II, I use law professors' turn to history and historians' reactions to it to investigate how lawyers and historians do their work. Chapter 6 is a report on how "the republican revival" became an "academic cottage industry." I also examine the debates between historians and law professors over republicanism and method arising from historians' attraction to historicism, context, change, and explanation and from lawyers' affinity for originalism, text, continuity, and prescription. In chapter 7, I suggest that history will remain an important form of constitutional argument and explore how lawyers, law professors, and historians can work together as activists toward shared objectives, including the defense of causes that legal liberals cherish.[18]

Such a strategy has pitfalls of its own. "Mandarin legal history," it focuses on what professors in elite institutions have thought about law. In reality, only a few law professors may have actually experienced the crisis of legal liberalism according to the terms described in my narrative. Nor have all those who suffered it tried to solve it by turning to other disciplines and to history. I submit, however, that those who have experienced it are sufficiently important to legal thought, the sense of crisis sufficiently widespread, and the turn to history sufficiently significant to warrant this book.

PART I

THE SPELL OF THE WARREN COURT

CHAPTER 1

TIMES TO REMEMBER

Although legal and political liberalism have been longtime allies, and legal realism affected both, they have had different careers. Unlike liberalism in politics and other disciplines, however, liberalism in law emerged from the 1960s intact. Only the question of rationalizing legal liberalism remained.

JOINED AT THE HIP: POLITICAL LIBERALISM AND LEGAL REALISM

When law professors write history, they mark legal realism as the jurisprudential divide between the old order and modernity. Adopting a "generous" definition of legal realism, William Fisher, Morton Horwitz, and Thomas Reed recently described the "heart" of the movement as "an effort to define and discredit classical legal theory and practice and to offer in their place a more philosophically and politically enlightened jurisprudence. All of the lawyers, judges, and legal scholars who contributed to that project should, in our view, be considered realists." By this view, Oliver Wendell Holmes marked himself as a realist when he declared that the life of the law was "not logic but experience," that the

Fourteenth Amendment did not "enact Mr. Herbert Spencer's Social Statics," and when he condemned classical legal thinker Christopher Columbus Langdell as the world's greatest living "legal theologian," whose "ideal in law, the end of all his striving, is the elegantia juris, or logical integrity of the system as system." The realists included not only such legal thinkers as Holmes and Felix Frankfurter but also Roscoe Pound, Benjamin Cardozo, and Louis Brandeis, along with law professors in the 1920s and 1930s who might have labeled themselves realists. Seen this way, Fisher, Horwitz, and Reed maintain, legal realism "set the agenda" for legal and, later, constitutional theory, by calling into question "three related ideals cherished by most Americans: the notion that, in the United States, the people (not unelected judges) select the rules by which they are governed; the conviction that the institution of judicial review reinforces rather than undermines representative democracy; and the faith that ours is a government of laws, not men."[1]

We might complain with John Schlegel, a historian of the realist movement, that this "big-tent" conception of realism and the realists conflates realism with an antiformalism that treats law as autonomous from society, and we might observe that most realists wrote almost nothing about public law. Yet the Fisher-Horwitz-Reed definition of realism I largely adopt in this book does illuminate one story that today's law professors, whatever their politics, tell about realism. And surely one reason the realists wrote so little about constitutional law was that they subscribed so fully to the antiformalist critique.[2]

Certainly the New Deal, which coexisted with legal realism, served as a political divide. Despite Herbert Hoover's best attempts to claim that he epitomized the liberal tradition, it was Franklin Roosevelt who gave "liberalism" popular meaning. "For the great majority of Americans, the word 'liberal' was literally born in the early New Deal." Instead of freedom from government, in the style of classical laissez-faire liberalism, Roosevelt spoke of liberalism in terms of freedom through government. Instead of "rights as freedoms" to be discovered, he thought in terms of "rights as claims" to be created.[3]

Alan Brinkley has chronicled the two stages of New Deal liberalism. During the Depression, liberals were concerned with the "critique of modern capitalism," especially "issues involving the structure of the industrial economy and the distribution of wealth and power within it."

Though practice did not always match rhetoric, the New Dealers defined social issues "almost entirely in terms of economics and class," maintaining that the "best hope for aiding oppressed minorities was economic reform." During World War II, this "reform liberalism" yielded to contemporary "consumption-oriented" and "rights-based liberalism," grounded on "a belief in the capacity of American abundance to smooth over questions of class and power by creating a nation of consumers" and dedicated to "increasing the rights and freedoms of individuals and social groups." Confident "that their new consumer-oriented approach to political economy had freed them at last from the need to reform capitalist institutions and from the pressure to redistribute wealth and economic power," liberals reconceived the role of government in the political economy. Relying on countercyclical spending to promote consumption and employment, the federal government would "create a compensatory welfare system (what later generations would call a 'safety net') for those whom capitalism had failed" and intervene more aggressively to protect individual and civil rights.[4]

Superficially, the New Dealers' faith in progress clashed with the legal realists' critical vision. Consider a staple of the realist corpus in the 1920s, "Legal Theory and Real Property Mortgages." In it Wesley Sturges examined three theories of mortgage law that logically led to different results. He showed that judges generally followed the three different paths to the same conclusion. Then Sturges analyzed the opinions of a randomly selected state court and proved that North Carolina's judges had not adhered to any one theory. State law was incoherent. "The point of the study was to demonstrate that the North Carolina law of mortgages made no sense and could most charitably be described as a species of collective insanity on the march," Sturges's student, Grant Gilmore, remembered later. Many of the realists agreed with Sturges that traditional and abstract legal categories or concepts, which isolated law from society, did not enable lawyers to predict the course of law.[5]

More generally, realists argued that classical legal thought ignored the indeterminacy of law and the role of idiosyncrasy in explaining judicial decisions. Their scholarship was in some respects traditional: it was doctrinal work, explicating the internal logic of legal rules and institutions and their relationship to other rules and institutions. Yet the realists saw that for each legal rule that led to one result, at least one more rule pointed toward another result. One realist said that legal rules and principles were "in the habit of hunting in pairs." Whenever judges confronted a doubtful situation, they would find that "in the past conflicting interest and conflicting social policies have each received recognition from the courts to some extent, and that these results have been rationalized in terms of 'conflicting' principles (or rules), each of which can easily and without departing from any prior decisions, be 'construed' as 'applicable' to the new case." By the realists' accounts, the doctrinal scholarship of traditionalists erred in treating law as a system of neutral rules that judges mechanically applied to reach the one legally "correct" decision. By pretending law was not socially constructed, classicists had imbued the rule of law with a false integrity.[6]

The realists debunked the rule of law as part of an effort to improve it. In undermining the predictive force of age-old legal rules, for example, realists often spoke of laying the groundwork for new ones. Their improved legal rules would utilize the insights of the social sciences and increase lawyers' proficiency at predicting the course of law. In using such rhetoric, realists sought to justify the place of the law school within the modern university, where Thorstein Veblen had declared that it no more belonged "than a school of fencing or dancing." Asked about his tenure as dean of Yale Law School, the center of legal realism after 1928, Robert Maynard Hutchins admitted to promoting realism because of his sense that a professional school's relationship to a university " 'had to' amount to more than simply 'sharing the same heating plant.' " Where traditional law professors exalted legal doctrine, realists spoke of "integrating" law with political science, economics, anthropology, sociology, and linguistics.[7]

The realists advocated a two-step program. They would expose both legal indeterminacy and judicial idiosyncrasy. While older legal scholars analyzed legal doctrine to demonstrate consistency, the realists' dissection of judicial decisions proved cases inconsistent and indeterminate. Having done that, the realists freed themselves to treat law as a tool of social policy and to look to the social sciences to define good policy.

Why the realists expected so much help from the social sciences was unclear. It may be, as some legal scholars now say, that the positivism, objectivism, and ethical neutrality of the social sciences at the time led realists to subordinate "political and moral passion to social science expertise." Perhaps, as some claim, the second step suppressed the radicalism of the first.[8] Further, though the realists made "law and social science" their mantra, they never got very far in their attempts to integrate the two. Nevertheless, they were the first generation of law professors to grapple with other disciplines and to demonstrate their importance to legal scholarship.

In part the realists did not advance their interdisciplinary agenda further because politics distracted them. However advanced their thought may have been and though realism predated the New Deal, most realists considered themselves political liberals. According to one of them, Jerome Frank, the realists made New Deal liberalism possible. They staffed the New Deal agencies that promoted reform and recovery. Legal realism proved the jurisprudential analogue of reform liberalism, and the realists became midwives to the birth of the contemporary constitutional order. Like the New Dealers, they tended to subordinate process to results. Both realists and New Dealers believed that human choice lay at the core of much private and public law. They characterized the distinction in classical liberalism between private and public law as arbitrary, demonstrating that all private transactions involved the state and that all law was, in an important sense, public law. They put their faith in the utility of social sciences. They employed an imaginative, modern, experimental approach to problem solving and to expanding the role of the welfare state.[9]

The realists also became devoted to the regulatory state, converting administrative law into "a vehicle for partisan objectives; for liberal partisanship." New Dealers were unimpressed by James Harrington's declaration that "a commonwealth comes to be an empire of laws and not of men." James Landis, a New Dealer who subscribed to much of legal realism, retorted that "good men can make poor laws workable," while "poor men will wreak havoc with good laws." By bringing the brightest to Washington to join regulatory commissions, New Dealers and realists hoped to ensure that a politically liberal, meritocratically selected elite would resolve disputes relating to the public good and advance the public interest.[10]

While their scholarship illuminated the judicial process, reflecting both their obsession with judging and the extent to which they identified with judges, realist law professors of the 1930s had little affinity for judicial activism as it was then practiced. "Indeed the rise of modern regulatory agencies was largely a product of a belief that the judiciary lacked the will, the means, and the democratic pedigree to bring about social reform on its own." Judicial activism had meant laissez-faire constitutionalism since the 1890s. The realists and New Dealers came of age in an era when the Court's decisions "seemed to be a road block to legislative developments . . . thought to be necessary for the decent humanization of American capitalism." Their hostility to the late nineteenth- and early twentieth-century Court far exceeded that of earlier modern American reformers. For realists and New Dealers, the paradigmatic case was *Lochner* v. *New York,* in which they believed Supreme Court members had gone out of their way to insist the rule of law "forced" them to reject social welfare legislation. For example, in declaring that law compelled them to strike down a centerpiece of the New Deal recovery program in *United States* v. *Butler* (1936), Justice Roberts pledged himself to textualism, expounding his infamous "T-square rule" of decision making: "When an act of Congress is appropriately challenged in the courts as not conforming to the constitutional mandate, the judicial branch of the Government has only one duty,—to lay the article of the Constitution which is invoked beside the statute which is challenged and to decide whether the latter squares with the former." The rhetoric intimated the majority believed itself constrained, but in fact, as Justice Harlan Fiske Stone charged in dissent, Roberts had "tortured" the Constitution to make it hostile to the New Deal. Others accused the justices of acting as "a superlegislature."[11]

With "the nine old men" of the Supreme Court seemingly on the verge of holding the entire New Deal unconstitutional, law professors who sympathized with Roosevelt's program acted. Harvard Law School professors Henry Hart and Felix Frankfurter, for example, attacked the Court in the law reviews. Following up on Frankfurter's suggestion, Hart also wrote a series of unsigned editorials in the *New Republic* alleging that Supreme Court justices such as Roberts couched reactionary results in neutral rhetoric. When Hart's exhortations against treating the Constitution as "the straitjacket for the status quo" proved unavailing, and Roosevelt proposed "packing" the Supreme Court by adding up to an additional six justices, Hart came out against Harvard University President James Bryant Conant with an argument for Roosevelt's Court packing plan. "If an evil exists, what solutions are possible other than President Roosevelt's proposal?" Hart asked. The majority of the Court was dissipating its prestige and influence by substituting its will for that of the lawfully elected representatives of the people. "Responsible men have earnestly to ask themselves whether the increasing popular dissatisfaction with the Court may not so undermine respect for the Court, and for all courts, as to threaten damage far exceeding anything which, by any calm view, may be anticipated from President Roosevelt's suggestion."[12]

In this showdown between the executive and judiciary, the Court blinked. Shifting course in 1937, it began upholding FDR's legislative program. The result of the 1937 showdown, according to political scientist Edward Corwin, was that the Court "discarded the idea that the laissez-faire, noninterventionist conception of governmental function offers a feasible approach to the problem of adapting the Constitution to the needs of the Twentieth Century" and began permitting the national government "to employ any and all of its powers to forward any and all of the objectives of good government." In the process, as Robert McCloskey said later, "many of the ancient myths which had long served as justifications for the Court's activities" were bruised. "Thereafter it was no longer possible for the judges and their supporters to take refuge from reasoned criticism behind the old incantations—the idea that the Court was merely the passive mouthpiece of an unambiguous constitution; the idea that the nature and range of the Court's power to intervene was settled once and for all by the Constitution itself or by unmistakable inferences from the Constitution." That was one lesson of 1937, although the realists had learned it long ago.[13]

Like their descendants, the realists did not all derive the same moral from 1937.[14] For members of the emerging legal process school, such as Hart, who remained a law professor, and Frankfurter, who was appointed to the Court in 1939, the moral was that the Court should take more seriously Justice Brandeis's admonition to use its power sparingly. Distinguishing between legislation and adjudication, they argued that the Court should respect the choices of the people's democratically elected representatives. It should show greater restraint, refraining from "imposing its own view of what the Country's good is." They did not believe, as Frankfurter said, that the Court they had claimed was a "superlegislature" when conservatives controlled it "should become a 'superlegislature' for 'our crowd.' " Legal process theory sought to explain "how respect for procedure and principled decision making might lead judges to outcomes that conform to institutional and democratic norms . . . develop a process explanation of law and adjudication that would achieve social purposes through the institutional settlement of disputes . . . [and defend] the view that right answers in legal decision making could be developed from a conceptual understanding of the institutional functions and competency of different governmental agencies of the legal system." For others, including some aging realists, the lesson was that the old Court had engaged in the wrong kind of activism. Instead of protecting property, they believed, the Court should focus on individual rights, which surged to the forefront of the liberal agenda during World War II. That obligation the Court seemed willing to contemplate undertaking, when in footnote 4 of *United States* v. *Carolene Products* (1938), Justice Stone proposed the Court uphold all reasonable economic legislation, while subjecting to stricter scrutiny legislation involving civil liberties and civil rights, which was particularly vulnerable "to perversions by the majoritarian process." Stone, who would soon become chief justice, now seized "the high ground of democratic theory" from advocates of judicial restraint by claiming that the defects of the majoritarian process created the need for judicial review. In claiming that judicial review furthered democracy by reconciling minority rights with majority rule, he set the Court in a new direction as activist as its old one.[15]

Footnote 4, then, did not make judicial review less idiosyncratic. By the time it was written, as George Braden said in a 1948 article entitled "The Search for Objectivity in Constitutional Law," Roosevelt's effort to pack the court and legal realism had helped change judicial parlance. "To talk, as Justice Roberts did, of simply laying a statute alongside an article of the Constitution to see if the former squares with the latter, now seems like dredging up an antiquity." Judges must have always known "that the judicial process is not that simple, that in the constitutional field the process is primarily political, not judicial; but it is only recently that they have admitted as much and have begun to discuss publicly their methods of deciding cases." Braden's readings of constitutional decisions convinced him that in the era after *Carolene Products*, the typical Supreme Court justice seemed to be saying: " 'I admit that Justice Roberts' mechanical method of squaring the statute and the Constitution was nonsense. Of course, we wield power. But this is potentially dangerous. Therefore, we must create a rule which is sufficiently objective to circumscribe us and our successors in our exercise of political power.' Thus the Supreme Court goes galloping off in search of objectivity." But to Braden, neither Stone nor any other justice had succeeded in finding it. For one example, Stone's thesis in footnote 4 appears to be something like this:

"I am first of all a man of reason. I believe in reason and its power in the market place of discourse. I am also a democrat. I believe that our governments are to be run by the governed. Therefore I shall use my great power as a Supreme Court justice sparingly, but I shall use it when it is necessary to preserve the democratic process or to protect those injured by unreason under circumstances where political processes, cannot be relied on to protect them. . . ."

This is not an objective theory of judicial review. The Chief Justice never claimed that it was. . . . It is perhaps unfair to set forth his thesis as an example of the effort to catch the will-o'-the-wisp of objectivity, but it does seem appropriate to present it as an early attempt to do the next best thing—i.e., to make an open declaration of personal beliefs.[16]

"To make an open declaration of personal beliefs"—was that the most realists would demand of judges? So the realists' critics believed. And because "the internal goods of constitutional adjudication" had been "respect for text and prior decisions, logical coherence and adherence to the norms of ordinary legal argument, freedom from partisan politics" since John Marshall's death in 1836, not everyone agreed with Braden that judicial candor was "the next best thing" to objectivity. In the context of the debate about relativism sparked by World War II, many antagonists read realists to say that idiosyncrasy swamped the rule of law altogether. More orthodox law professors ridiculed them for espousing a "gastronomic jurisprudence," which explained judicial decisions on the basis of what judges ate for breakfast. At the very least, opponents warned, the realists' focus on the subjectivity of the decisional process "gave even the most offensive Nazi edict the sanction of true law." Traditionalists branded the realists as nihilists and excoriated them for preaching Holmes, Hobbes, and Hitler. Where the realists espoused ethical pluralism, their antagonists saw ethical relativism.[17]

PLURALISM, PROCESS, AND THE

"COUNTER-MAJORITARIAN DIFFICULTY"

Amid the revulsion against dictatorship in the aftermath of the war, an emphasis on democratic process, sometimes in a transparently political "apolitical" fashion, spread across the American intellectual landscape. In 1939, Clyde Kluckhohn had characterized cultural relativism as "probably the most meaningful contribution which anthropological studies have made to general knowledge." In the 1950s, anthropologists Alfred Redfield and A. L. Kroeber found universal values. "They suggested not only that there are general standards of judgment that transcend cultural boundaries, but that the moral standing of primitive societies is below that of civilizations like the United States," which exalted free speech. So, too, abstract expressionism in the postwar era "was full enough of alienation and anxiety, and expressive enough of violent fragmentation and creative destruction (all of which were surely appropriate to the nuclear age) to be used as a marvellous exemplar of US commitment to liberty of expression, rugged individualism and creative freedom. No matter that McCarthyite repression was dominant, the challenging canvas of Jackson Pollock proved that the United States was a bastion of liberal ideas in a world threatened by communist totalitarianism."[18]

Literature reinforced that message. Just as the realists were reproached for gastronomic jurisprudence, so Cleanth Brooks complained that "almost every English professor is diligently devoting himself to discovering 'what porridge had John Keats.' This is our typical research: the backgrounds of English literature." Brooks and others who subscribed to the New Criticism shifted the focus to structure, irony, tension and ambiguity. "Reading poetry in the New Critical Way," Terry Eagleton said later, "drove you less to oppose McCarthyism or further civil rights than to experience such pressures as merely partial, no doubt harmoniously balanced somewhere else in the world by their complementary opposites." By decontextualizing literature, the New Critics promoted a "benign pluralism" suited to the new crop of university students of all classes who lacked the common values their prewar counterparts learned in prep schools.[19]

At a time when America perceived itself at danger from without, historians and political scientists made that benign pluralism characteristic of their nation in past and present. "While only a few years earlier, the relativity of value threatened to disarm democracy, the same relativism now became the theoretical foundation for free government." In a world where ethical values always changed, ensuring that interest groups fought them out through a fair process became more important than guaranteeing specific outcomes.[20]

In the early twentieth century, Progressive historians such as Charles Beard had concentrated on presenting America's history as a battle between the classes and the masses. At a time when decisions such as *Lochner* enraged reformers, the Constitution came in for an especially hard time; Beard claimed that instead of "working merely under the guidance of abstract principles of political science," the Founders labored for "distinct groups whose economic interests they understood and felt in concrete, definite form through their own personal experience with identical property rights." According to him, "protection of property rights lay at the basis of the new system," and the "crowning counterweight to 'an interested and over-bearing majority,' as Madison phrased it, was secured in the peculiar position assigned to the judiciary, and the use of the sanctity and mystery of the law as a foil to democratic attacks." The Constitution represented a counterrevolution. His contemporaries had hailed Beard "for undermining the patriotic banalities of nineteenth century historiography." Beard, however, was no longer blessed. For the historians, sociologists, and political scientists of the 1950s who sought to displace the Beardian, or Progressive, paradigm, the salient point was the consensus, rather than the conflict, between Americans.[21]

Indeed consensus allegedly made the United States unique. In explaining the absence of socialism in the United States and the reason for "American exceptionalism," Louis Hartz painted a picture of an America born free, rich, and modern. There individualism, pluralism, economic self-interest, capitalism, and natural rights had long predominated. "Here is a Lockian doctrine which in the West as a whole is the symbol of rationalism, yet in America the devotion to it has been so irrational that it has not even been recognized for what it is: liberalism," Hartz wrote in *The Liberal Tradition in America,* his reinterpretation of American thought. "There has never been a 'liberal movement' or a real 'liberal party' in America: we have had the American Way of Life, a nationalist articulation of Locke which usually does not know that Locke himself is involved." Locke's preeminence explained "the unusual power of the Supreme Court and the cult of constitution worship on which it rests. Federal factors apart, judicial review as it has worked in America would be inconceivable without the national acceptance of the Lockian creed, ultimately enshrined in the Constitution, since the removal of high policy to the realm of adjudication implies a prior recognition of the principles to be legally interpreted." The "fixed" and "dogmatic" philosophical, or classical, liberalism which accounted for America's "moral unanimity" did not bar political liberalism. "Indeed, as the New Deal shows, when you simply 'solve problems' on the basis of a submerged and absolute liberal faith, you can depart from Locke with a kind of inventive freedom that European liberal reformers and even European socialists, dominated by ideological systems, cannot duplicate."[22]

Though a poignant tone suffused Hartz's presentation of Locke as proto-Babbitt, his contemporaries in the mid-1950s celebrated the Constitution, continuity, and consensus as interdependent. Hailing the American Revolution as a "Revolution without dogma . . . a prudential decision taken by men of principle rather than the affirmation of a theory," and stressing the "continuity of American political thought," Daniel Boorstin jubilantly explained why Americans lacked enthusiasm for Fascism, Nazism, or Communism. "We have actually made a society without a plan. Or more precisely, why should *we* make a five-year plan for ourselves when God seems to have had a thousand-year plan ready-made for us?" Daniel Bell applauded "the end of ideology." For Bell, the word *ideology,* which he defined as "a hardening of commitment, a freezing of opinion," and "the conversion of ideas into social levers," reeked of the left. He insisted that the old ideologies, "particularly Marxism," had become "exhausted" in the West by midcentury. Once dangerous mobs were blamed for having led their countries down the road to totalitarianism, scholarly enthusiasm for "the people" disappeared.

As Robert Wiebe said, the citizen became "democracy's weak link," the "public psyche" a thing of horror. The goal was to keep government out of the hands of citizens. For those writing articles with titles such as "In Defence of Apathy," declining voter turnouts were good news; they freed the elites to safeguard democracy. Political scientists such as David Truman pointed to the role of interest groups with overlapping memberships in serving "as a balance wheel" in the United States. Truman emphasized that despite "polite fictions," pressure group politics affected the judiciary, "inevitably a part of the political process," as well. The Constitution and Founding Fathers became fashionable again. Seymour Lipset's *The First New Nation* made the Constitution the key to "stable democracy"; Reinhold Niebuhr declared it the Founders' purpose to preserve "democratic stability." To Niebuhr and Lipset, democracy *was* stability.[23]

Potitical scientist Robert Dahl tried to steer a middle road between Madison and the people. He stopped just short of placing Madison "in the camp of great antidemocratic theorists," and he challenged the notion the Constitution was important to "democratic theory," which Dahl defined as the "processes by which ordinary citizens exert a relatively high degree of control over leaders." Dahl was no more positive, however, about populism, which he thought focused on the goals of "political equality and popular sovereignty" to the exclusion of all else. Elections rarely indicated majority predilections, he said. Many people did not vote, and those who did were not necessarily endorsing their candidates' policies: "the essence of all competitive politics is bribery of the electorate by politicians." Elections did, however, "vastly increase the size, number, and variety of minorities, whose preferences must be taken into account by leaders in making policy choices." And it was "this characteristic of elections—not minority rule but minorities rule" which distinguished democracies from dictatorships. Where the fear of majority tyranny led Madison to constitutional checks and balances, Dahl acclaimed "minorities rule" as the answer. "If majority rule is mostly a myth, then majority tyranny is mostly a myth too. For if the majority cannot rule, surely it cannot be tyrannical." Dahl's "American hybrid" of "polyarchal" democracy concentrated on the "social" checks and balances pluralism provided. Its key feature, government by minorities, might cause "frustration as minorities thwarted each other," but at least it foreclosed dictatorship and ensured balance and stability. In this system, the Supreme Court functioned as "policy-maker and legislator in its own right." Hardly "the *deus ex machina* that regularly saves American democracy from itself," the Court generally followed election returns, though sometimes it took its time about doing so. As they had operated in the past and would continue to function, constitutional rules had not guaranteed "government by majorities or . . . liberty from majority tyranny. . . . Constitutional rules are mainly significant because they help to determine what particular groups are to be given advantages or handicaps in the political struggle." In America, as nowhere else in the world, and "to an extent that would have pleased Madison enormously," governmental decision making was "the steady appeasement of small groups. . . . Decisions are made by endless bargaining." The American political system was a "strange hybrid," Dahl concluded, but it proved "a relatively efficient system for reinforcing agreement, encouraging moderation, and maintaining social peace." Pluralism became an end in itself, polyarchy the best way of achieving it. Where the New Dealers envisioned pluralism serving liberalism and social justice, Dahl saw only pluralism.[24]

Even John F. Kennedy got into the act. At his Yale University commencement speech in 1962, he proclaimed that Americans had entered an era of "more subtle and less simple" domestic problems. "They do not relate to basic clashes of philosophy and ideology, but to ways and means of reaching common goals—to research for sophisticated solutions to complex and obstinate issues." The age demanded the technocrat.[25]

Harvard Law School's Mark DeWolfe Howe hinted in 1953 that a Supreme Court decision holding segregation unconstitutional would mesh nicely with the pluralist vision of balancing interest groups. Yet pluralism's emphasis on the importance of interest-group jostling only underscored the belief of some legal scholars, particularly Howe's colleagues at Harvard, that the Supreme Court should serve a different and purer function. Horse trading might happen in the legislature or executive, but they saw little place for it in the judiciary. They viewed the notion of "judicial politics" as normatively oxymoronic. In the words of later legal scholars, legal process theorists thought the Court should be "the forum of principle," a place where the goal of "maximizing the total satisfaction of human wants" was pursued, as in popularly elected governmental branches, but where process and precedent were taken seriously, legal craft coveted, and cases decided according to law, regardless of who got what, when, and how. The popularity of the legal process idea in the postwar era reflected not only a reaction against legal realism, but also law professors' determination to prevent the pragmatism of pluralism from infecting the judiciary. As Neil Duxbury said, process theorists viewed jurisprudence "as quality control. . . . Different organs have different tasks to perform within the legal process; and it is for students and scholars not only to identify those tasks but also to ascertain whether or not they are being performed properly."[26]

Brown v. *Board of Education* tested such inspectors. It was fuzzy. Beyond declaring school segregation unconstitutional, what exactly did the opinion do? Did it put an end to segregation or require integration? Further, the opinion seemed self-consciously realist: devoid of constitutional analysis, it relied in part on sociological data and did not attempt to demonstrate that the Fourteenth Amendment's framers intended to outlaw school segregation. Nor did the Court actually say it was overruling the key precedent standing in the way of *Brown*—*Plessy* v. *Ferguson* (1896). That decision, legitimating segregation in railway cars, had found the doctrine of "separate but equal" consistent with the Fourteenth Amendment's equal protection clause and said that segregation did not stamp African Americans with a "badge of inferiority." While *Brown* left the sense *Plessy* was no longer good law, Chief Justice Warren evaded the question of whether *Plessy* was correct at the time it was decided and implicitly distinguished *Plessy,* hinting that since *Plessy* involved intrastate travel, it was not really germane. In addressing segregation in the schools, the Court could not "turn the clock back to 1868 when the Amendment was adopted, or even to 1896 when *Plessy* v. *Ferguson* was written," he insisted. Because of changed circumstances, the Court had to address public education "in light of its . . . present place in American life throughout the Nation." Observing that "[t]oday, education is perhaps the most important function of state and local governments," Warren noted that it was "the very foundation of good citizenship." The state had decided to provide education, and it must make that opportunity "available to all on equal terms." Regardless of whether the separate facilities were "equal" to those afforded whites, segregation of children in public schools on the basis of race deprived "the children of the minority group of equal educational opportunities." Contrary to "psychological knowledge" at the time of *Plessy*, contemporary social science showed that school segregation did make African Americans feel inferior. "Any language in *Plessy* v. *Ferguson* contrary to this finding is rejected." The Court concluded that "in the field of public education the doctrine of 'separate but equal' had no place. Separate educational facilities are inherently unequal." *Plessy* was "inapplicable to public education." A remedy came later: the following year, in *Brown II*, the Court simply required that desegregation take place with "all deliberate speed."[27]

We still cannot be certain of how the Court went about deciding *Brown*. Influenced by the imprint Frankfurter had left on the archives and on his clerks, those who first reconstructed the case tended to present Frankfurter as its hero: he had stalled a decision until unanimity was possible, he had ensured unanimity by separating the decision segregation was unconstitutional in *Brown I* from the decree indicating when segregation had to end in *Brown II*, and he had devised the gradualist desegregation formula in *Brown II*. A quarter-century after *Brown*, one law professor wrote: "In some sense, all of constitutional theory for the past twenty-five years has revolved around trying to justify the judicial role in *Brown* while trying simultaneously to show that such a course will not lead to another *Lochner* era." That certainly set out the challenge as Frankfurter wanted others to believe he had articulated it.[28]

But as Frankfurter's star dropped in the law school world after the late 1960s, other histories of the case appeared. They suggested that the only justice in *Brown* deeply bothered by the specter of 1937 was Frankfurter and that he ensured unanimity only in the sense that he devised a formula that would enable him to go along with his brethren. Frankfurter apparently believed that by proceeding slowly with school desegregation, and remaining silent about segregation outside the schools— above all, about the sensitive southern miscegenation laws preventing intermarriage between the races—the Court would win the compliance of "respectable" southerners. If these histories are correct, he was a poor prophet. Southerners rejected *Brown*, and Frankfurter's inconsistency may have only made them less likely to comply with it. Further, as Mark Tushnet said, Frankfurter's "innovation, 'all deliberate speed,' when coupled with southern resistance, transformed constitutional law" by disconnecting the right abridged from the remedy. By this account, justices Black and Douglas had prescribed a traditional remedy—requiring "immediate desegregation, in the sense that every child who applied to attend a desegregated school with room for him or her would have to be admitted, knowing full well that where resistance was likely to be strongest, few parents would subject their children to the inevitable ordeal." Frankfurter resisted, and ironically, the gradualist formula the Court ultimately adopted "made the Constitution a mere instrument to accomplish socially valuable ends, not a commitment to the immediate vindication of fundamental—present and personal—rights. Moreover, it encouraged the federal courts to see themselves as managers of social transformation," legitimating "the very activism" Frankfurter had feared.[29]

Frankfurter also made *Brown* a tough case for some of his followers. In the words of Gerald Gunther, "Frankfurter, despite his general avowal of a restrained position on judicial review . . . was given to expediency, discretion, and manipulation in the interests of prudence and avoiding political attacks on the Court." Of Frankfurter's protégés, only his former clerks, Alexander Bickel and Harry Wellington, both of whom became professors at Yale, seemed to understand and share their mentor's prudentialism, which would have restricted the Court's intervention in controversial political issues to vital occasions. "No good society can be unprincipled; and no viable society can be principle-ridden," Bickel contended. "[W]ould it have been wise at a time when the Court had just pronounced its new integration principle, when it was subject to scurrilous attack by men who predicted that integration of the schools would lead directly to 'mongrelization of the race' and that this was the result the Court had really willed, would it have been wise just then . . . on an issue that the Negro community as a whole can hardly be said to be pressing hard at the moment, to declare that the states may not prohibit racial intermarriage?" he asked publicly regarding the miscegenation issue. As Gerald Gunther observed, the young Alexander Bickel stood for "100% insistence on principle, 20% of the time." Bickel, who declared it judges' duty to extract fundamental principles and values "from the evolving morality of our tradition," later admitted he had never dealt successfully with one criticism of his work—that "the whole thing boils down to a disagreement about results and a certain personal distrust you have for these judges, the only additional thing being, perhaps, that you don't think they have been very skillful in expressing themselves." Taking Frankfurter's pose more seriously, other members of the legal process school—a group that included Henry Hart and Albert Sacks of Harvard, Herbert Wechsler of Columbia, Philip Kurland of Chicago, and Judge Learned Hand—treated Frankfurter as the symbol of judicial restraint and the integrity of the legal process he pretended to be. Like Bickel, most process theorists had been trained at Harvard, and as Bickel complained to Frankfurter, those who stayed on in Cambridge to teach often sounded "a little priestly." Process theory attracted both theologians and prudentialists, the apostles of consistency and those willing to accept inconsistency.[30]

Some scholars have maintained that *Brown* "produced a sharply critical reaction among elite legal thinkers, for it challenged at the deepest levels their effort to re-establish a neutral, value-free system of constitutional doctrine." Gary Peller placed the process theorists of the 1950s within the mainstream of the benign pluralist consensus of that decade. Acknowledging that they were "by and large liberal reformist in their political outlook," he alleged that with respect to questions of public law, they placed their faith in a "procedural freedom symbolized by free speech and open inquiry" and refused "to take a stand on substantive social issues."[31]

That indictment seems harsh. Process theorists were, of course, obsessed with procedural issues, with limiting the role of the federal courts, with ensuring courts found and followed statutory purpose, and with developing "the boundaries for the institutional competence of the judiciary when acting in the special role of judicial review," what Hart called "the morality of function." Though Hart and Sacks never published their casebook on the legal process, Hart and Wechsler's *The Federal Courts and the Federal System* (1953), dedicated to Felix Frankfurter, is "probably the most important and influential casebook ever written." It is also true that process theorists, such as Hart, Sacks, and Wechsler, never successfully integrated *Brown* or other key Warren Court decisions with either their vision of the legal process or their narrow and intricate conception of federal jurisdiction. In one of his own more theological moods, Frankfurter once sent Hart a cartoon of a boy standing at the blackboard telling his teacher: "O.k., o.k.! So two and two equals four—let's not make a Federal case out of it!" Treating the "Court as protector of human rights," Frankfurter grumbled in an accompanying note, meant "Ter Hell with jurisdiction!" Appropriately, the Warren Court opinion that apparently alienated Hart most was *Baker* v. *Carr,* the jurisdiction case Warren considered his most significant, and which may have given Frankfurter a stroke.[32]

Yet for *Brown* what stands out is the lengths to which process theorists went to justify it or to set out broader and more consistent grounds on which it could have rested. Though no one knew for sure what constitutional principles underlay the opinion, from the beginning, "[a]cceptance of *Brown*" by law professors operated as an "admission ticket for entry into mainstream constitutional dialogue." A student who heard Hart hold forth against *Baker* v. *Carr* told him: "You easily (I might say hurriedly) distinguish *Brown* v. *Board* whenever it is brought up as precedent." In his Supreme Court "Foreword" for the 1953 *Harvard Law Review,* Sacks, a former clerk for Frankfurter, said of *Brown:* "The outstanding feature of the decision lies in the triumph of a principle—a principle which the Court must have found to be so fundamental, so insistent, that it could be neither denied nor compromised. The principle can be easily stated: the Constitution requires equal treatment, regardless of race." Separating the declaration that segregation was unconstitutional from the decree setting out the remedy did not trouble Sacks: that, he said, was an act of "judicial statesmanship." Nor was he bothered by the fact that southerners might dislike the opinion. "It seems fair to reply that even in those states, there exists an inner, unexpressed sense that segregation and equality are like oil and water, even though it is accompanied by an equally strong feeling that segregation is nevertheless essential." Perhaps that inner sense might not win out in the electoral process, but it was "relevant to the problem before the Court, a politically sheltered institution whose function it is to seek to reflect the sober second thought of the community." Sacks queried the Court's extension of *Brown* to strike down segregation outside the schools in a series of summary per curiam opinions without explanation. (He did so with good reason. As one scholar wrote some forty years later: "*Never* did the Court get around to informing the nation of the legal basis for desegregating the South, outside the context of education," and it was not until 1963 that the Court "finally announced that a State may not constitutionally require segregation of public facilities.") Yet Sacks raised his question in the most tentative manner. More confidently, he stressed "the need for fuller statements" of the views of the Court in his discussion of per curiams in general. "At stake is the value which the Court handled so carefully and so well in the *Segregation Cases,* the acceptability of the Court's decisions to the lower courts and to the Bar as a whole." Sacks thus tried to remove *Brown* from the arena of responsible criticism of the Court.[33]

For his pains, Sacks received a letter from his former boss. Quoting Sacks, Frankfurter wrote: " 'The principle can be easily stated; the Constitution requires equal treatment regardless of race.' Really!? Are you overruling the Civil Rights cases [of 1893, which prevented Congress from taking affirmative steps to combat racial discrimination and from outlawing private discrimination]? Is all this bother about F.E.P.C. [Fair Employment Practices Commission] redundant and wasteful in that the Constitution itself already contains a F.E.P.C.?" Had Sacks become so entrenched in the academy that he had forgotten that "a summary disposition may be indicated in cases where there might be easy agreement about the result but not by the roads for reaching it, in short, where there is difficulty about the very statement you want"?[34]

Chagrined, Sacks replied that he "had no intention of suggesting that the Fourteenth Amendment goes beyond state action," a position still too broad for Frankfurter, and insisted that hiding disagreement did little to help the Court as an institution. "The explanation of per curiams in terms of differences among the justices may seem quite natural to the justices, but I don't think it can fully satisfy the outsider. It affords virtually complete immunity to criticism for failure to explain. . . . I have had letters from two lawyers both of whom won their cases this past Term on per curiam opinions, both of whom felt that the Court was not justified in being so cryptic." On receiving this letter, Frankfurter immediately "risk[ed] being deemed academic"—a charge to which the onetime Harvard professor unashamedly" pled guilty—by circulating his correspondence with Sacks to his colleagues on the Court. "Sacks' comments are worthy of consideration because, unlike much that is written even by law professors regarding the Court's work, Sacks' reflections are highly informed and sophisticated." The episode was typical of Frankfurter, who routinely used his law professors' letters and articles as conduits through which to exhort his brethren on the bench to produce better-reasoned decisions.[35]

In *Brown,* however, Frankfurter's efforts misfired. He regarded *Brown* as a special case in which the Court's action had been appropriate. Behaving pragmatically, he tried to circumscribe the impact of the case among those disinclined to support action. In 1955 and 1956, he twice persuaded the Court to dismiss *Naim* v. *Naim,* which would have raised the constitutionality of state laws against miscegenation, on "a make-weight excuse." In doing so, he ran the risk of consuming *Brown* with some of the fires he had helped set. At a time when Frankfurter was trying desperately to shore up the legitimacy of the Court, he alienated the theologians who would otherwise have supported *Brown* and its progeny on the very grounds he himself so often publicly and privately criticized other Warren Court opinions—inconsistent reasoning. Gunther's biography of Learned Hand, for example, demonstrates that Hand injected criticism of *Brown* into his 1958 Holmes Lectures at the last minute and that he would have accepted *Brown* had he been allowed to interpret it broadly. Obsessed with the desire to win over the South, however, Frankfurter convinced Hand that "the somewhat opaque *Brown* opinion . . . was an education case and that the permissibility of racial discrimination in other areas had to be decided by context-specific, case-by-case balancing analysis." To Hand, if *Brown* applied just to education, it was a substantive due process case. Under Frankfurter's hammering, Hand concluded that the Court "had not meant to propound an absolute rule against racial inequality but instead engaged in its own reappraisal of legislative judgments." Therefore, and though he spoke at the time of the Little Rock crisis—"the greatest crisis over school desegregation since *Brown* was decided"—at a time when the Warren Court's "efforts at dismantling the widespread institutionalization of attacks on civil liberties during the McCarthy era" were also under attack, and at a time when, for the first time since the Civil War, Congress was threatening to reduce the Court's appellate jurisdiction, Hand not only queried the legitimacy of judicial review, but also rejected judicial activism on behalf of all "preferred freedoms" except the First

Amendment, and specifically criticized *Brown* as judicial legislation. Ironically, Hand's original interpretation of *Brown* may have correctly stated what the justices had in mind and might have made clear, but for Frankfurter's intervention in the opinion-writing process.[36]

The following year, another veteran of the "early decades of this century, [when] judicial activism had meant 'anti-progressivism,' " Herbert Wechsler, used his Holmes Lectures to criticize the reasoning in *Brown,* "an opinion which is often read with less fidelity by those who praise it than by those by whom it is condemned. The Court did not declare, as many wish it had, that the Fourteenth Amendment forbids all racial lines in legislation." He maintained that its opinion simply subordinated one constitutional value, freedom of association of whites facing integration, to another, freedom of association of African Americans suffering segregation. Wechsler added that he took "no pride" in saying the procedural grounds on which the Court had dismissed *Naim* were "wholly without basis in law." He later explained: "My point was that a judge is obliged, insofar as he deals with the extrapolation of a particular constitutionally protected value, to give it an even-handed development."[37]

Wechsler's article was reprinted in the same issue of the *Harvard Law Review* as Henry Hart's "Time Chart of the Justices," which criticized the Court "as essentially a voice of authority settling by virtue of its own ipse dixit the questions that duly come before it. This conception unhappily seems to underlie some of the Court's own actions, as when it decides opinions which do not explain, or decides important questions without any opinion whatever." Hart called on the Court to leave more time for "the maturing of collective thought," concluding "the time must come when it is understood again, inside the profession as well as outside, that reason is the life of the law and not just votes for your side." When Wellington wrote Hart "that a judicial position which is unable to embrace and approve the Supreme Court's action in *Naim* v. *Naim* . . . is not a fully matured philosophy" and that any decision of the merits in *Naim* "would have seriously undercut the effectiveness of the Supreme Court's segregation decision" and "might seriously have threatened the Court as an institution," Hart was unimpressed. The "question is whether a court is ever justified in giving a false reason in order to avoid facing up to an embarrassing issue," Hart replied. "This view may seem to you excessively unworldly. But I am able to persuade myself that worldly as well as unworldly considerations support it. Segregation is ultimately a moral issue, and the moral authority of the Court is one of the principal instruments we have for getting rid of it. I do not think that it makes good sense to let that sharp edge of the instrument get blunted."[38]

Such declarations left little doubt about where Hart's heart lay. Like Hand's correspondence with Frankfurter, they were private, but, with the exception of Hand, scholarly commentators were generally publicly sympathetic to *Brown*. Process theorists joined other, more activist law professors, such as Charles Black, who asked, "How long must we keep a straight face" when "we are solemnly told that segregation is not intended to harm the segregated race, or to stamp it with the mark of inferiority?" Together, the two groups made *Brown* sacred. In the lead article of the 1955 *Harvard Law Review,* Bickel argued that "the direct and noble march to the Court's conclusion in the Segregation Cases" was not precluded by the original understanding of the Fourteenth Amendment. The historical record, "properly understood, left the way open to, *in fact invited,* a decision based on the moral and material state of the nation in 1954, not 1866." In 1956, Charles Fairman used the increasingly prestigious annual "Foreword" to the *Harvard Law Review*'s discussion of the previous Supreme Court term to evaluate "the principal criticisms" of *Brown,* all of which he found wanting. He concluded: "It is futile to make war 'to keep the past upon its throne.' " Even those who were skeptical of the opinion's reliance on sociological data, such as Edmond Cahn, saw *Brown* as a victory for "the whole American people." Further, law professors' reaction to Hand underlined the extent of their pro-*Brown* sympathies. Privately, Hart raged at Hand's "obtuseness," complaining "What he . . . seemed to me to be saying in his lectures . . . is that at bottom law and the social order reflect nothing but a struggle among contending classes. The most striking thing in this analysis is the total failure to recognize the existence of any principles of social order which are independent of the appetites and wills of the contending groups." Responding to Hand publicly, Wechsler vowed his allegiance to *Brown* as the decision with "the best chance of making an enduring contribution to the quality of society of any that I know in recent years" and defended judicial review. Gunther observed that "the rare praise" Hand received for the Holmes Lectures "came from the South." Otherwise, "the reception of Hand's message proved almost universally negative. . . . The academics' response was equally predictable. Most of them were supporters of the Warren Court; even those who had doubts tended to suppress them in the face of the more obvious evil of assisting the reactionary critics during a time of political crisis."[39]

Other decisions of the Warren Court were not off limits, however. Process theorists did seek to "integrate a tamed realism back into the mainstream of legal thought" by emphasizing "institutional competence," calling for "reasoned elaboration of judicial decisions," and attempting to separate law from politics, process from substance, fact from values. Even its defenders would admit that except in the case of *Brown*, process theorists generally did favor the status quo, employing a "thin theory of democracy," which subordinated substance to procedure and did not make "substantive fairness . . . a primary element of political legitimacy." The prototypical process theory charge that the Court's sloppy craftsmanship, subjectivity, and activism threatened its future was prominently featured in the 1957 *Harvard Law Review*. In an attack on Douglas's majority opinion in the recent *Lincoln Mills Case* and a hymn to Frankfurter's dissent there and craft skills in general, Bickel and Wellington declared that scholars' duty was to "defend the Court against ill-intentioned nonsense which comes decked out in legal trappings," but added that could not mean a moratorium on responsible criticism of the Court. They continued: "The Court's product has shown an increasing incidence of the sweeping dogmatic statement, of the formulation of results accompanied by little or no effort to support them in reason, in sum, of opinions that do not opine and of per curiam orders that quite frankly fail to build the bridge between the authorities they cite and the results they decree." Quoting this critique, Hart's 1959 "Foreword" warned "that these failures are threatening to undermine the professional respect of first-rate lawyers for the incumbent Justices of the Court, and this at the very time when the Court as an institution and the Justices who sit on it are especially in need of the bar's confidence and support." Wechsler likewise called on the Court to reach "principled" decisions resting on reasons "that in their neutrality and generality" transcend "the immediate result that is achieved."[40]

Wechsler later explained that he was not developing "a formula to guide or produce the decision of hard cases, but rather . . . a negative test, which would force the judge to ask himself, 'Would I reach the same result if the substantive interests were otherwise?'' ' His contemporaries misunderstood him. They thought he had advanced a positive test, somehow injecting neutral principles with substance. As he admitted, they perceived him to have denounced realism.[41]

Writing in 1963, Bickel, "the most influential scholar of his generation in the field of constitutional law," made no bones about expressing his opposition to activist judicial review and realism. After eight years of the Warren Court, Bickel was pessimistic about judicial power. The Founding Fathers had "invited" judicial review, he conceded in *The Least Dangerous Branch*. They had "specifically, if tacitly, expected" the Court to review the constitutionality of other branches of government, both federal and state, and Chief Justice John Marshall had followed their wishes when he justified judicial review in *Marbury* v. *Madison* with the lame explanation that "the *writtenness* of the Constitution and . . . its supremacy in cases of clear conflict with ordinary law" gave the Court "what is nowhere made explicit in the Constitution—the ultimate power to apply the Constitution, acts of Congress to the contrary notwithstanding." Bickel noted that no one would disagree with Marshall's proposition that a court could not allow a legislative "act repugnant to the Constitution" to stand when that act conflicted with the Constitution. "But Marshall knew (and, indeed, it was true in this very case) that a statute's repugnancy to the Constitution is in most instances not self-evident; it is, rather, an issue of policy that someone must decide. The problem is who." Marshall's opinion "begged the question-in-chief." Bickel demolished the "props" for judicial review Marshall had provided, demonstrating that they were both "frail" and "too strong. . . . Literal reliance on *Marbury* v. *Madison* may lead to a rampant activism that takes pride in not 'ducking' anything." Had Bickel been a historian, his inquiry might have ended with some observations about motivation. Since Bickel was a law professor, however, and unashamedly viewed the enterprise of scholarship as more normative than explanatory, he argued with the Founders about their wisdom.[42]

"The root difficulty" with judicial review, Bickel proclaimed, is that it "is a counter-majoritarian force in our system." Bickel had little use for the Founders' effort to make popular sovereignty meaningful. When Alexander Hamilton claimed in *Federalist 78* that judicial power was not superior to legislative power, reasoning "that the power of the people is superior to both; and that where the will of the legislature, declared in its statutes, stands in opposition to that of the people, declared in the Constitution, the judges ought to be governed by the latter rather than the former," Hamilton, according to Bickel, had been using the word *people* as "an abstraction. Not necessarily a meaningless or a pernicious one by any means; always charged with emotion, but nonrepresentational—an abstraction obscuring the reality that when the Supreme Court declares unconstitutional a legislative act or the action of an elected executive, it thwarts the will of representatives of the actual people of the here and now; it exercises control, not in behalf of the prevailing majority, but against it." For that reason, "the charge can be made that judicial review is undemocratic." With these words, Bickel assured the revival of the "majoritarian paradigm" in constitutional theory.[43]

Though Bickel had worked to isolate pluralism from the judiciary, he now went further, seeming to reject pluralism itself. For he not only quarreled with the Founders, but also queried the political theorists of his generation. Oddly, at a time when they were exalting the Constitution for stabilizing democracy, dismissing the individual citizen, and proclaiming the impossibility of majority rule, Bickel apparently equated democracy with majoritarianism. Democracy meant "a representative majority" had the power to make and reverse decisions, he emphasized. Nothing political scientists said could "alter the essential reality that judicial review is a deviant institution in the American democracy." Even assuming Dahl had correctly identified "minorities rule" as the alternative to majority rule, "it remains true nevertheless that only those minorities rule which can command the votes of a majority of individuals in the legislature who can command the votes of a majority of individuals in the electorate." Somehow or other, in elections and the legislative process, "the minorities must coalesce into a majority." Nor was Bickel swayed by political theorists, such as David Truman, who pointed to the impact of interest groups on the judiciary. Such writers had shown that the electoral process was not the only way of ensuring responsiveness of government to the governed, and that by extrapolation, "judicial review, although not responsible, may have ways of being responsive." Yet the ultimate responsiveness of the Court to public opinion was not sufficient to justify judicial review. "[N]othing can finally depreciate the central function that is assigned in democratic theory and practice to the electoral process; nor can it be denied that the policy-making power of representative institutions, born of the electoral process, is the distinguishing characteristic of the system. Judicial review works counter to that characteristic."[44]

Bickel's concept of democracy was both populist and simplistic. "For me," he explained to Eugene Rostow, judicial review was "not democratic, unless we so play with that word as to drain it of all content." Without any evidence, Bickel assumed that the legislature pursued a majoritarian perspective, reflective of the popular will. His legislature, like that of other process theorists, rationally and pragmatically pursued the public interest. Without any evidence, he assumed that the public could identify well-reasoned opinions, and that they would bolster popular faith in the rule of law. Further, in focusing on *Marbury*, Bickel had chosen an easy target. He glossed over important cases in the development of judicial review, such as *McCulloch* v. *Maryland*, which used judicial review as a means toward the goal of achieving federal supremacy over the states, and in which, Bickel himself admitted in passing, Marshall had gone "beneath the bland proposition advanced in *Marbury* v. *Madison*." As the subject matter of *McCulloch* would suggest, Bickel also downplayed the role of federalism in necessitating judicial review. While many instances of judicial review involved separation of powers and the Supreme Court against Congress, or individual rights against government, surely national supremacy was also important to the Founders. As Holmes put it, "the United States would not come to an end if we the Supreme Court lost our power to declare an Act of Congress void," but it might "if we could not make that declaration as to the laws of the several States." The Founders apparently foresaw judicial review could assist in establishing the relationship of the national government to the states, as well as strengthen the authority of state courts against popular majorities. As it developed, judicial review did help to resolve conflicts between federal and state government before and after the Civil War. "And," as the historian Jack Rakove emphasized, "this in turn should have mitigated the countermajoritarian dilemma, to some degree, especially as it would or should have been perceived in the wake of *Brown,*" when the authority of the national government was challenged throughout the South. Nevertheless, Bickel had spoken, and suddenly democracy "became a central legitimating concept in American constitutional law," and "democratic legitimacy" a concept threatened by judicial review.[45]

As Bickel knew, inside the law school world little he said was new. Law professors and judges had been mocking *Marbury* and worrying about the undemocratic nature of judicial review since the time of Thayer and Holmes. Still, Bruce Ackerman and Michael Klarman rightly credited Bickel with the "classic statement" of the problem. The words he used to sum it up, "the counter-majoritarian difficulty," were epigrammatic.[46]

Ironically, within pages of introducing that epigram, Bickel came around to the pluralist view that judicial review *was* democratic. Instead of following Marshall or the *Federalist,* however, he justified judicial review by proclaiming it the Court's role to pronounce and guard public values in principled fashion and to build consensus around them. On some occasions, such as *Brown,* whose specter haunted *The Least Dangerous Branch* and epitomized "all that I have tried to say about the role of the Supreme Court in American government," he emphasized, the Court did need to inject "itself decisively into the political process." Such occasions were "relatively few," the Court must bank its prestige for them, and having acted, it must "foster assent, and compliance through consent." Bickel applauded *Brown II* and the "all deliberate speed" formula precisely because it represented such an attempt. For even on the rare occasions the Court appropriately intervened in the political process, its law could not ultimately prevail "if it ran counter to deeply felt popular needs or convictions, or even if it was opposed by a determined and substantial minority and received with indifference by the rest of the country. This, in the end, is how and why judicial review is consistent with the theory and practice of political democracy." Readers paid less attention to that language, however, than they did to Bickel's explication of "the charge" that judicial review was undemocratic. To them, Bickel seemed to be heralding a return to the bad old days before 1937 when judicial review and democracy were antagonists.

Yet while he questioned the partnership between judicial review and democracy that Stone had tried to establish in *Carolene Products,* Bickel made judicial review and democracy only potential, rather than actual, antagonists. That was still quite an accomplishment: henceforward, the hypothesis that constitutionalism was antithetical to both justice and democracy haunted constitutional law.[47]

At the same time, Bickel reviled legal realism as a "cry of nihilism," claiming it constituted "cynicism pure and simple." According to him, the realists contended there was no such thing as a principled decision. Therefore legal realism provided no criteria for identifying how to reach a decision and no basis for justifying the power of the Court in a democracy. Bickel was unfair, for realism did not necessarily lead to the wholesale judicial activism he condemned. Sometimes it did; at others, it did not. The whole point of realism was that the person wielding the theory was more important to how matters turned out than the theory itself. As Bickel himself acknowledged ever less uneasily as he grew older, the realist tradition had produced his own prudentialism, as it had spawned the other "scholastic mandarins" who rapped the legal reasoning by which Warren Court opinions justified decisions. The criteria process theorists applied in evaluating the Court's success—"instrumental effectiveness, institutional self-regard, and public acceptance"—themselves reflected realism's imprint. Sometimes, one critic said, process theorists almost seemed to exalt an "image of a Supreme Court holding aloft a collective moistened finger to test the drift of popular preference."[48]

What united process theorists such as Wechsler, Bickel, Kurland, Sacks, and Hart was the belief judges had too fatalistically accepted judicial (in)discretion. Haunted by the memories of the conservative Court in the early twentieth century and threatened by Stalinism, such legal scholars sought to domesticate realism, constrain judges, and separate law from politics. Stressing that limits to judicial discretion did exist, they concentrated on the methods by which judges did and should reach decisions. Judges, Hart said, should recognize their duty to articulate and develop "impersonal and durable principles." They could leave the horse-trading to legislators. The job of judges was to promote respect for the rule of law.[49]

Process theory, which in part represented an attempt to indict the

Warren Court's more lamely articulated decisions, urged judges to spotlight the reasoning and craft techniques of the legal profession in their opinions. In so exhorting, process jurisprudents searched for a constitutional theory that would reinforce the integrity of the legal process, enable judicial decisions to transcend results, justify the negotiated document the Court had produced in *Brown,* and reduce worry about the counter-majoritarian difficulty. They never found it.[50]

In fact, frequently neutral principles and process theory led to a peculiar sort of doctrinal scholarship. It was easy to parody student notes of the era. All one need include, the editors of the *Harvard Law Review* said in another context later, was "a takeoff on lines such as these: ' . . . Thus, it appears that traditional bright line rules should no longer serve as guides for adjudication in this area. Rather courts should base their determinations on a functional balancing of the relevant interests.' " So the doctrinal work of process theory's patron saint, Justice Frankfurter, and the scholarship of the law professors allied with him could be mocked. Even Bickel acknowledged judges had to choose among "enduring values." Yet the very act of balancing might leave "far too much to the individual judge's predilection." Neutral principles were all well and good, but they did not guarantee neutral attitudes toward the principles. Balancing simply underlined the extent to which those who subscribed to process theory accepted realism's revelation of the role of idiosyncrasy in the decisional process. Meanwhile Frankfurter's retirement in 1962 enabled the Warren Court fully to embrace judicial activism.[51]

GLORY DAYS

It was the Warren Court of 1962–69 that became "a cultural phenomenon." That was the Warren Court which "came into its own as an independent political actor." During that period, Lyndon Johnson and Earl Warren reintroduced and expanded on the New Dealers' vision of political liberalism, linking it to legal liberalism. "To be a liberal . . . meant favoring a stronger role for the state in the economy, moderate redistribution of income, state action to improve the lot of the disadvantaged, legal protection for the accused and mentally ill, and legal bans on racial discrimination," law professor David Trubek explained.

To be legalist meant maintaining the "faith in law as an instrument of progressive social change." Legalists, such as Johnson and Warren, assumed that "most of the 'flaws' in American society could and would be corrected through legal means. They had faith in the immanent liberalism of legal institutions and equated 'law' with 'freedom' and 'equality.' " There was a foreign policy dimension to their program as well, which entailed "exporting democratic capitalism." Johnson's Great Society entailed social and economic reform at home and globalism abroad to preserve capitalism and to fight poverty and injustice.[52]

In its heyday between 1962 and 1969, the Warren Court adopted Johnson's politics. Mark Tushnet rightly labeled the Warren Court an element of Johnson's Great Society coalition. The Court's legal liberalism consisted of political liberalism and judicial activism in equal parts. The Warren Court "gave us reason to believe that state activism was a constitutional duty," Owen Fiss recalled. In the words of the journalist Anthony Lewis, the Warren Court's record confirmed "an implausible idea, temperamentally and historically . . . a revolution made by judges." Its decisions reflected an insistence on what Hannah Arendt called "a right to have rights." Opinions emphasized "the importance of individual dignity, the significant role of the modern state in creating and maintaining the good society, and the importance of shaping the relationship between the modern welfare state and the individual so that the state's powers are not imprudently diminished, and individual dignity is preserved." The Court expanded civil liberties and civil rights, while assiduously avoiding a decision on the constitutionality of the Vietnam War and invalidating some of the most eloquent protest against it.[53]

The Court made liberals happy for it dodged the tension between liberty and equality. Justices did so by using liberalism's language of individual rights and freedom to help children, the disenfranchised, non-Christians, suspected criminals, minorities, and the poor. Sub silentio, they took "the group perspective on the victim." Horwitz later described the Warren Court as "the first Court in American history that really identified with those who are down and out—the people who received the raw deal, those who are the outsiders, the marginal, the stigmatized." Expanding equal protection analysis beyond race, Warren Court justices declared a number of rights "fundamental." (In one notorious instance, they even made the right to interstate travel a fundamental right, while refusing "to ascribe the source of this right . . . to a particular constitutional provision.") The Court also revamped the relationship between state and federal courts by opening up federal courts to those likely to be mistreated in state courts. "Barriers to the federal courts came tumbling down . . . to provide a sympathetic forum for the enforcement of rights that genuinely *ought* to be enforced against majoritarian power." And the Court tried to promote social justice throughout the states by nationalizing the Bill of Rights.[54]

To its detractors, of course, what the Warren Court called "constitutional interpretation" was "legislation from the bench." "Perhaps some of you may detect, as I think I do, a return to the philosophy of St. Thomas Aquinas in the new jurisprudence," Justice Brennan told an audience during a 1965 speech on the role of the Court. "Call it a resurgence, if you will of concepts of natural law—but no matter." One commentator responded: "But no matter?!?!?!" Though Anthony Lewis might celebrate Warren as "the closest thing the United States has had to a Platonic Guardian, dispensing law from a throne without any sensed limits of power except what was seen as the good of society" and relish the feeling of being "present at a second American Constitutional Convention" on the day the Court announced its one person–one vote rule and demanded reapportionment of state legislatures, other observers wondered who would guard the guardian. They agreed with Justice Harlan, who warned that decisions such as one person–one vote "give support to a current mistaken view of the Constitution and the constitutional function of this Court. This view, in a nutshell, is that every major social ill in this country can find its cure in some constitutional 'principle,' and that this Court should 'take the lead' in promoting reform when other branches of government fail to act." Critics griped that the Warren Court was "a continuing constitutional convention and a joint session of Congress rolled into one." As Fred Graham said, "the gusto" with which Warren Court justices went about changing the law "struck some people as being unseemly."[55]

Since some of the Warren Court's most enthusiastic activists had been legal realists, judicial activism now became associated with legal realism. To skeptics among law professors, no one on the Court exemplified the realist-gone-amok more than William O. Douglas. In the 1965 case of *Griswold* v. *Connecticut,* for example, Douglas cobbled together a constitutionally protected right to marital privacy, though the Constitution never mentioned privacy. The rights enumerated in the First, Third, Fourth, Fifth, and Ninth Amendments and applied to the states through the Fourteenth Amendment, he reasoned, had "penumbras, formed by emanations from those guarantees that help give them life and substance." *Griswold* could have rested on other grounds. Justice Harlan's concurrence developed an alternative rationale for a constitutional right to privacy, based on substantive due process, arguing that "the Fourteenth Amendment's due process clause protection of 'liberty' represented a substantial limitation on state action wholly independent of the specific constitutional guarantees spelled out in Amendments One through Eight." As one who had come of age during the constitutional crisis of 1937, however, Douglas would have none of that because he thought it represented a return to *Lochner*.[56]

To Warren's clerk John Hart Ely, both Harlan's reliance on substantive due process and Douglas's implication of a right to privacy in *Griswold* constituted dangerous judicial activism. "Instead, Ely suggested, the Chief Justice should look at *Griswold* and how the [1879] Connecticut statute [which criminalized the use or prescription of contraceptives by women and their doctors] prevented the operation of birth control clinics for the poor, but not the provision of similar services to better-off patients of private physicians, in the light of an eighty-year-old equal protection decision, *Yick Wo* v. *Hopkins*." In that case, the Court had announced, "Though the law itself be fair on its face and impartial in appearance, yet, if it is applied and administered by public authority with an evil eye and an unequal hand, so as practically to make unjust and illegal discriminations between persons in similar circumstances, material to their rights, the denial of equal justice is still within the prohibition of the Constitution." Unlike federal courts and other state courts, which had read a "medical exception" into laws such as Connecticut's outlawing contraceptives (permitting physicians to prescribe contraceptives for married women), the Connecticut supreme court had ruled in 1940 that the statute included no implied medical exception. The statute posed no problem for married women who could afford private medical care, because physicians violated it with impunity. But after the Connecticut supreme court's ruling, all birth control clinics in Connecticut had promptly shut down for twenty-five years. Warren ignored Ely's advice, and the equal protection clause analysis was buried in an individual concurrence.[57]

Griswold, a due process case in right to privacy clothing, did not represent the Warren Court's usual approach toward decision making. Nor was Douglas the first member of the Court to ply "penumbras" or the last to resort to "penumbral reasoning." Nevertheless, to legal scholars at the time, *Griswold* seemed typical of Warren Court reasoning, and some groused that no matter what the opinion said, it really represented a return to *Lochner*. The term "unprincipled penumbralist" became synonymous with "realist," "liberal," and "judicial lawlessness."[58]

Some Warren Court opinions did make no pretense of suggesting law and legal theory compelled the justices to reach their decision. In fact, Mark Tushnet thought that "constitutional theory played a rather small role during the height of liberal activism." He pointed out: "Earl Warren had humane instincts, not a systematic philosophy." "Yes, Counsel, but is it fair?" Warren reputedly asked the lawyers who argued before the Court. One popular quip described the apparent thought of the Warren Court majority: "With five votes, we can do anything."[59]

Consider the case of Justice Abe Fortas. A legal realist and New Dealer in the 1930s, he became Douglas's ally and a Great Society liberal in the 1960s. Fortas sometimes wrote draft opinions without legal citations in them, then ordered his law clerks to "decorate" them with the appropriate legalese. That did not mean that Fortas knew the supporting law was there. It meant that he considered law indeterminate and did not care about it much at all. In his hands, realism licensed crude instrumentalism. As one of Fortas's biographers, I found his cavalier attitude toward the rule of law surprising. Since I usually liked the results he reached and since historians explain more than they diagnose, however, his approach and the Warren Court's activism posed no political or professional problems for me.[60]

But the subjectivity of Fortas's opinions and those of his Warren Court colleagues led more principled scholars, particularly the law professors who persisted in doctrinal research and who made their living by analyzing the Court's output, to ask why the Court should possess so much power in a democracy. At Harvard Law School in the 1960s, Morton Horwitz remembered, "it was common to mock Warren for often asking from the bench whether a particular legal position was 'just.' Sophisticated legal scholars did not speak that way."[61]

"Sophisticated legal scholars" believed they must show that legal and constitutional doctrine underlay judicial opinions. Otherwise, they would be doomed to spend their professional lives presenting the opinions as smoke screens for judges' economic, social, personal, and political preferences. That task could be left "to a notable school of historians and political scientists who decline to see the legal process as anything more than a chintz cover for the thrust of sheer power and will." If they did not take judicial opinions seriously, academic lawyers feared they would undermine the integrity of the rule of law. Herbert Wechsler never lost his wonder at those who thought that "the credibility, authority, and power of the federal judiciary is an asset that can be extended to the moon without any loss anywhere." Some law professors worried that respect for the legal process would disappear if the public came to believe America's was a government of men, not law.[62]

The process theory critique, which grew out of legal realism, hurt the legal realism associated with the Warren Court, not legal liberalism. It did not demonstrate dissatisfaction with the Warren Court's results, for almost all law professors at the time were liberal in their politics. "Perhaps the most striking feature of the commentary of the 1950s and 1960s was that the participants battled so fiercely about whether the Court could or should act, while agreeing so fundamentally on the substantive goodness of what the Court was doing or would do if not restrained by its own modesty." Wechsler picked the cases he criticized in his Holmes Lecture because he admired their outcomes. "It seemed more powerful, more persuasive, and morally preferable to exhibit the tension between results and bases, in terms of situations where I liked the result, but felt a moral obligation to question the grounds than to take the easy cases where I disliked the result and undertook to question the grounds," he said. "Indeed, one of the elements of rhetorical effectiveness in the piece was precisely that I persuaded people that I liked the results and still felt it important to question the grounds." Similarly, Bickel, who had a soft spot for the Warren Court's criminal justice decisions, wrote Frankfurter about the opinion preventing state courts from admitting evidence obtained in violation of the Fourth Amendment: "I can't help liking the results (I don't *want* to be reasonable) but what a messy process."[63]

In the 1960s, then, two groups of law professors bickered, but theirs was a family quarrel between Warren Court activists and process theorists, two wings of the realist tradition. Old realists suggested that in their "illusive . . . quest for legal certainty," process theorists were creating "a false faith in judicial objectivity," which would "cripple the exercise of creativity and reinforce the status quo." Arnold claimed process theorists would be satisfied when Supreme Court justices came only from the ranks of those trained by the "dialecticians" at Harvard Law School. Others influenced by realism, such as Charles Black and Eugene Rostow, more tactfully suggested that judicial review protected and enhanced democracy. Echoing Stone, they insisted that judicial review was necessary to protect oppressed minorities from majority tyranny. Black, a "judicial activist proudly self-confessed," imaginatively focused on the "structures and relationships created by the constitution in all its parts or in some principal part," maintaining that "the status of citizenship" alone legitimated the Court's civil rights and First Amendment decisions, and stressing that it "would be wrong not to see in the work of the Warren Court as a matter of net thrust, an affirmation—the strongest, by a very long interval, in our whole history—of the positive content and worth of American citizenship." Still other legal scholars gave themselves to the Court, writing elaborate apologias explaining why the Court had to act as it did. For members of this group, comprised largely but not exclusively of the young, the counter-majoritarian difficulty did not pose a problem when a Court so obviously hoped to further democracy and social justice. Their interest was in how the Court should act. Another group, made up mainly of individuals who remembered the conservative Court before the constitutional crisis of 1937, tempered praise for Warren Court consequences with concerns over whether the Court should act and fears that sloppiness, when the Court did act, hurt judicial legitimacy.[64]

Like Kurland, the Court's most vociferous critic, Bickel did become more doubtful about political and legal liberalism as the decade progressed. But in 1968, Bickel gave himself "heart and mind" to Robert Kennedy, describing him as "our best hope" and suggesting that "his fine and passionate instincts were leading him back to the older, enduring strains in the American liberal tradition—strains that for me are identified with Brandeis." In the summer of 1969, Bickel was still writing favorably of the Warren Court in the *New Republic*.[65] "Compared to the references to the breakdown of American civilization that are strewn through his later works, Kurland's criticisms of the Warren Court [as late as 1970] are small jabs indeed." Mostly united in favor of the social change the Warren Court sought to make, law professors disagreed over the means it used.[66]

The Warren Court made the 1960s a good time for the law schools. All aspects of society—even corporate law firms—seemed viable candidates for reform. Law professors "moved easily between the practical and academic worlds." Through their students and scholarship, they could even believe they ran the world. Some legal scholars became involved in the law and society movement. Their empirical studies reflected their hope for "a union of objectivist knowledge and progressive politics." Such work reflected the faith in scientific models as objective foundations for progress that marked the postwar era. It drew on the social sciences to identify gaps between legal rules and realities and to advance "the liberal legal agenda of the day." Under what circumstances was the impact of legal doctrine "defeated, diverted, or distorted by social forces in need of reform"? Other professors stuck with analyzing the Court's opinions. Their doctrinal scholarship made a difference, they believed. "The growing incidence of law review material cited in Supreme Court opinions is testimony of the extent to which legal writers have influence upon the Justices," one legal liberal wrote in 1965. Still other law professors, such as Thomas Emerson, fought the good fight in the courtrooms. Such individuals had impact: Harry Kalven noted that the Warren Court's opinion expanding First Amendment rights in *New York Times* v. *Sullivan* echoed Weschler's brief on behalf of the newspaper. Charles Reich could dazzle liberals and transform the law by making a broad policy argument for expanding property rights to include entitlement to benefits distributed by the welfare state, in an article that would win the most citations in the history of the *Yale Law Journal* and help to propel the Court's procedural due process revolution.[67]

If Warren Court decisions contributed to the decline and destruction of the Great Society, just as Great Society legislation itself did, so much the better. The right's demonization of Warren for his Court's expansion of individual and civil rights only helped matters. "People are afraid of saying anything that can be misused by the Faubuses and Byrds," who supported segregation, Bickel said privately of law professors in 1958. In the 1960s, the Warren Court attracted even more fire, becoming an issue in the 1964 and 1968 elections. Congress even attempted to over-rule some of the Court's criminal decisions by enacting the Omnibus Crime Control and Safe Streets Act in 1968. Because of the intensity of the reaction against it, the Warren Court continued to foster solidarity among academics who joined in support of it. Annoyed that his law professors were not saying the Warren Court at high tide "made the Nine Old Men look by comparison like a collection of juristic angels," Frankfurter once told Bickel that "you law professors really should sharpen your pens so that there is no mistaking as to what the trouble is and where the blame lies." They were generally not as harsh as Frank-furter would have liked. For all Bickel's insistence in personal corre-spondence that he "generally functioned without regard to the question of aid and comfort" to enemies of the Warren Court and that he could not "bring myself to call a moratorium on criticism of the judicial pro-cess, whenever I think, as I most often currently do, that the results are agreeable to me," he vigorously defended the Court and its members in the *New Republic* whenever they were attacked in Congress. Philip Kur-land recognized that the Court had "been most fortunate in the enemies that it has made, for it is difficult not to help to resist attack from racists, from the John Birch Society, and from religious zealots who insist that the Court adhere to the truth as they know it." He saw that "the 'pas-sivists' who condemn the Court for its activist role are always in the vanguard of those who rush to the defense of the Court when it is at-tacked for its activism."[68]

For all Harvard's mockery of Earl Warren's way of asking questions, members of a new generation who went to law school during the Warren years and entered law teaching at Harvard and elsewhere during the 1960s—a group including Jesse Choper, Bruce Ackerman, Ronald Dworkin, John Hart Ely, Owen Fiss, Frank Michelman, and Lawrence Tribe—were not haunted by memories of the old Court and viewed judicial activism even more tolerantly than did their teachers. True, the editors of the *Harvard Law Review* might sarcastically say that "[a]t least a few of the current law school generation, some readers may be surprised to hear, have not in their approval of the Warren Court's reforms entirely forgotten a lesson of the judicial crisis of the 1930's: the warning that a judiciary acting like a Council of Revision in favor of either right or left poses great institutional dangers." Yet those very editors also criticized the form process theory had taken. "Emphasis on principled, restrained adjudication is commonly associated with a great tradition of scholars and judges often connected in some way with the Harvard Law School," they observed, noting that Frankfurter, Hart, and Bickel, among others, had all studied law at Harvard and served on its law review:

> Even to those of us who share their concern for principle, there has sometimes seemed to be too much emphasis on durability and not enough on development. The compelling logic of the Frank-furter-Hart school has often appeared to impose a deadening hand; one has felt impelled to choose between rejecting progress-ive judicial positions for lack of coherent, principled rationales and abandoning the commitment to principle in frank undisguised result-orientedness.[69]

Most Harvard students chose progressivism. They worried, for example, that Hart did not notice "the air of jubilation among many law students this morning, caused by the Supreme Court decision in *Baker v. Carr*." One student wrote Hart: "With all respect, I am completely confident that Baker v. Carr is right—and you are wrong." In 1969, the editors of the *Harvard Law Review* dedicated an issue to "Chief Justice Earl Warren who with courage and passion led a reform of the law while the other branches of government delayed." Their counterparts at the law school's student newspaper called on lawyers "to refuse to advance the interests of those things which worsen rather than alleviate the problems of our society," and described the 1960s as "a unique and wonderful age of judicial activism, where the courts have often been ahead of other governmental agencies in attempting to solve the pervasive problems of our society." Fiss, a Harvard law student in the 1960s who went on to clerk for Justice Brennan, insisted that "even in those days it was understood that Harvard did not speak for the profession as a whole, and even less so for the young, who looked to the Court as an inspiration, the very reason to enter the profession."[70]

Among students at other law schools, there were few signs of ambivalence about the Warren Court. Law schools capitalized on the Warren Court. "Glossy admissions brochures entice some students into law school with promises that lawyers of the future, riding white chargers, will crusade against social problems," one student wrote. As a law student working with prisoners at Leavenworth, another future academic learned "that the federal courts are special. They are the most splendid institutions for the maintenance of governmental order and individual liberty that humankind has ever conceived." To the children of the Warren Court, "the law seemed like a romance." The editors of the *Yale Law Journal* said Earl Warren "made us all proud to be lawyers." Alexander Bickel, who deplored the "vision of courts and of the law as instruments for millenarian social change" that brought so many to law school, might remind students that "federal judges were not inevitably 'little Earl Warrens in black robes,' " but he did not produce many "little Alexander Bickels in blue jeans." A red diaper baby who attended Yale in the 1960s, such as Mark Tushnet, would be aware of the many voices claiming that "the experience of the Warren Court and its interaction with the civil rights movement convinced us that, notwithstanding the skeptical determinism associated with Marxist social theory, it was possible for law to become an autonomous force for progressive social change." As one of his contemporaries emphasized: "We did not notice that there were many more clouds in that promising sky than we realized." The president of the *Stanford Law Review* spoke hopefully of infusing the "law, long dominated by traditional motives of security and avarice" with "altruism and self-sacrifice." Judge Skelly Wright concluded "that one of the greatest legacies of the Warren Court has been its revolutionary influence on the thinking of law students. . . . [F]or them, the Supreme Court *was* the Warren Court. For them, there was no theoretical gulf between the law and morality; and, for them, the Court was the one institution in the society that seemed to be speaking most consistently the language of idealism which we all recited in grade school."[71]

A "small but articulate minority of law students" and an occasional professor on the left might claim the Court's lack of position on the Vietnam War meant "our judges are neither bold nor courageous when evil comes full-blown." They might also grumble that for all its expansion of civil liberties, the Warren Court supported the state's power to police dissent in cases involving protest against the war. Like other political and legal liberals, Warren Court members saw a dichotomy between the state and the individual, and they did not always side with the individual. A few outsiders may have seen, too, that the Court's expansion of individual rights and national government did little to foster the left's ideal of community.[72]

But complaints were rare, and generally less forceful than the critiques of Warren Court liberalism for providing "half a loaf," which originated from outside the law schools. No law professor on the left in the 1960s produced as biting a critique of Warren Court liberalism as that written by historian Howard Zinn. Even his critique of the Warren Court paled next to the left's critique of political liberalism and Lyndon Johnson in the 1960s. In launching one of the early salvos against "the myth of rights," political scientist Stuart Scheingold nevertheless stressed that the "civil rights experience provides the clearest demonstration that legal tactics . . . can release energies capable of initiating and nurturing a political movement." As late as 1979, one scholar wrote in *Telos:* "Contemporary left-wing critics of American institutions either ignore the Supreme Court, or accept the liberal view of it. That view, particularly as applied to the Court during Warren's Chief Justiceship (1953–1969), is that the Court was benign, that it acted as a counterweight to oppressive measures of the 'political' branches, that it did not participate in 'cold war' policies, that its major decisions had nothing to do with economic developments, and that its influence has been highly 'progressive.' "[73]

The law schools remained apart from the revolution—in large part because their inhabitants perceived law to be in the vanguard of the revolution. Further, one law professor said, "There were very few elementary or secondary students in the S.D.S., on the one hand, and even fewer law students, Supreme Court clerks, or junior faculty [at law schools], on the other hand." Another law professor acknowledged that the "student revolts that have rocked campuses across the country have left the law schools relatively untouched."[74]

Certainly, the key word was "relatively." Yale Law School briefly housed a "commune" in its courtyard, but when ten thousand people converged on New Haven for the Black Panther trials in 1970, Yale law students focused on opposing "any attempt to stop the trial of the New

Haven Panthers by extralegal or coercive means" and on ensuring their right "to receive a fair trial." Bickel remarked thankfully that "training still tells a little." After Martin Luther King's assassination, *Harvard Law Review* editors likewise intoned that King's "militant nonviolence . . . has left lawyers and public officials with a precious opportunity: to channel the action and passion of our time into legal change now, before the processes of the legal system for orderly resolution of social disputes become largely irrelevant." For the editors of the *Columbia Law Review,* King's death made it even "more important" that "all [lawyers] admit a professional as well as civic obligation to find specific ways" lawyers could help solve "society's problems." Though law students at Harvard struck in 1969, class attendance increased during the strike, and the dean noticed that "law students did not seem to be preoccupied by ROTC, expansion or the other issues debated in the university." Instead they pointed to problems other law school deans liked to think worst at Harvard. The *Harvard Law Record* noted that at an all-night law library study-in, "a suggestion that the study-in discuss the eight demands of the Harvard College strikers was hooted down in favor of a free-flowing give-and-take session on grading, evaluation and alienation at Harvard Law." These issues seemed tame in an era when students in other parts of the university were claiming "with great sonority . . . that the university is an employer, a landlord, a lender, and is thus as prone to exploiting the disadvantaged as is any profit-making enterprise; that the alleged mutualities of knowledge do not exist in the ordinary classroom, where things-to-be-learned are authoritatively superimposed on passive, sullen, and unwilling learners, nor do they exist in the library and the laboratory, where research is in service to the status quo; that professionalism is not at odds with the urge to self-advantage, but a sophisticated method of indulging it, through guild controls and restrictive licenses; that academic freedom is a shibboleth, first because it is not practiced, as the preponderance of safe opinions among scholars testifies, and second because it is not practicable, since the involvements of the university with society are so *ex parte* that the very call for institutional neutrality is itself a disingenuous form of partisanship." Liberalism fared better in law than it did in other fields.[75]

Elsewhere, the compromises of liberalism, the breakdown of "law and order," and the war in Vietnam tarnished the concept by decade's end and led to disciplinary change. Radical sociology grew out of dissatisfaction with the sociologists who supported the war. Rejecting the theory that society was grounded on consensus, one graduate student wrote an essay "entitled, as I recall, 'Karl, Come Home, All is Forgiven,' which expressed my discovery of the power and basic truth of Marxian analysis." In linguistics, the generative semanticist James McCawley, who sometimes adopted the pseudonym Quang Phuc Dong, founded "the *Fuck Lyndon Johnson* school of example construction." In literature, accusations of "political complicity or irrelevance" toppled the New Criticism. "In the 1968 charge on the Modern Language Association convention, one could all but hear echoing from the marbled halls of the old Hotel Americana a version of Wordsworth's cry to Milton: 'England has need of thee, / She is a fen of stagnant waters.' "[76]

Radical historians read their disenchantment with liberalism back into the past. Some turned their backs on the consensus school and intellectual and political history, discovering social history. "If undergraduates could have voted in a binding referendum on the war, peace would have arrived the day after," Paul Buhle reasoned. "Beyond teach-ins, demonstrations, educational agitation, and downright riots, what remained?" The emergence of women's history, black history, and labor history represented, in part, "a search for allies" in America's past. Historian David Hackett Fischer would condemn presentism as "the mistaken idea that the proper way to do history is to prune away the dead branches of the past, and to preserve the green buds and twigs which have grown into the dark forest of our contemporary world." Presentism, however, had long characterized some good historical work, and now it led some radical historians to showcase "the struggles of the past in order to enhance prospects for struggles of the present."[77]

While the new social historians were writing history "from the bottom up" and often through the Marxist prism of class, other colleagues kept the spotlight on "elite manipulation." Some historians now claimed that the New Deal had given the disenfranchised a raw deal. William Appleman Williams and his students decried "corporate liberalism." Buhle stressed that those "two words passed overnight into the national vocabulary: they formed an especially suitable description for a Democratic leadership that steered an almost reluctant military establishment toward a land war in Asia. The phrase seemed to explain the hitherto unexplainable; it responded to a need for understanding that was instinctually felt by tens of thousands of dissenters who were unable to place themselves on any standard political map."[78]

Political scientist Theodore Lowi echoed the dissatisfaction with liberalism. In *The End of Liberalism,* he contended that the 1960s exposed the weakness of an "interest-group liberalism" built on the "flawed foundations" of pluralism. According to Lowi, 1960s liberals had wrongly decided to fight poverty. The phenomenon they confronted was "the injustice that has made poverty a nonrandom, nonobjective category." They should have attacked injustice and worked "to change social rules and conduct in order that poverty become and remain a random thing, an objective category. The interest-group-liberal approach—defining the effort as economic, attaching it to the welfare system, and making it almost totally discretionary—was not merely superfluous and redundant; it produced a whole array of unhappy consequences." Liberal governments would never achieve justice. The War on Poverty had only "diverted attention from civil rights" while leaving the old rules intact. In the end, liberalism was *conservative.* Historians John Blum and Richard Hofstadter had made the same point in the 1950s when they described reform as a way of avoiding revolution, but Lowi's words were redolent of a sinister, conspiratorial elite. He had "deliberately" picked the word "conservative," Lowi said, "because it best evokes a sense of the very things to which . . . liberalism claimed to be most antagonistic." Yet though Lowi condemned "liberal jurisprudence," he associated it with the regulatory process, which pitted interest groups against each other, not Warren Court judges.[79]

Through all of this, the Warren Court shone. Law professors, many of whom had clerked at the Court, celebrated the greatness and courageousness of Warren and his colleagues when Earl Warren surrendered the chief justiceship to Warren Earl Burger in 1969. By the time new courses in poverty law appeared, and Nixon's invasion of Cambodia and the disaster at Kent State had made "political authority . . . so suspect and the danger of civil disorder so great" that "the very basis of the American democracy" was imperiled, Warren was gone. In retirement, he seemed wiser than ever. "We have had many crises in prior years, but none within the memory of living Americans which compares with this one," Warren observed.[80]

Years later, one of his faculty hosts recalled Warren's visit to the University of California, San Diego, in the fall of 1970, a year after his retirement as chief justice:

> [A] huge crowd of students, faculty, and San Diegans packed the quadrangle of John Muir College to hear Warren's talk. As he rose to speak, several students unfurled a large banner from a nearby balcony. A hush fell over the throng, most of whom expected the worst in student graffiti, perhaps "F—k the Chief Justice." Our campus and hundreds of others across the nation had been rocked by student strikes in April when President Nixon launched the invasion of Cambodia. At Kent State and Jackson State, national guardsmen and state troopers had gunned down protestors. Earl Warren, former Chief Justice of the United States, represented the Establishment. But instead of an expletive, the banner read, "Right on, Big Earl!" The crowd roared its approval. Warren flashed a broad grin and proceeded to deliver a scathing attack on those who believed the country could have law and order without social justice.[81]

Even after Kent State and Cambodia, the editors of the five-year old *Harvard Civil Rights–Civil Liberties Law Review* reaffirmed their faith in making "law an effective instrument for advancing the personal freedoms and the human dignities of the American people." Similarly, Michael Tigar's critique, in his 1970 *Harvard Law Review* "Foreword," of the small world that Supreme Court justices occupied espoused continuing the Fifth Amendment work the Warren Court had "begun in *Miranda*," and nostalgically invoked "a sense of injustice, informed by past Court decisions." The Warren Court became "judicial Camelot."[82]

Despite Warren's retirement, then, the Warren era continued. As it did, it seemed clear that legal realism had not fared as well as legal liberalism. Legal realism had become too closely associated with the judicial activism that underlay the Warren Court's liberalism. As with pornography, Warren and his colleagues might know justice when they saw it.[83] But to many legal scholars, it seemed that the Warren Court had not produced objective criteria for justice. With a chief justice in power who might not pursue the politics of the Warren Court or law professors, legal realism now seemed dangerously unprincipled.

The politics of the Burger Court were not exactly clear. On the basis of some of its decisions, some commentators suggested that the Warren era lasted until 1974, and at one point Mark Tushnet even suggested renaming the Warren Court the Brennan Court. "The Brennan Court decided all the central cases of the Warren Court except *Brown* v. *Board of Education,* which the Brennan Court enthusiastically endorsed and extended. The Brennan Court went on to decide *Roe* v. *Wade,* and the gender discrimination cases as well."[84]

But by that analysis, the Warren Court's legacy appeared to be the "rootless activism" or "Lochnering" the Burger Court practiced in the 1970s—a constitutional theory of fundamental rights, and decisions, such as *Roe,* the "classic example of judicial usurpation and fiat without reason." Legal scholar Philip Bobbitt attributed "the universal disillusionment with *Roe* v. *Wade* . . . to the unpersuasive opinion in that case." In the five years following *Roe,* Lawrence Tribe of Harvard developed three different justifications for its outcome, none of which had much to do with the majority's reasoning. Many other law professors tried to find another doctrinal home for *Roe* as well: Richard Posner described the case as "the Wandering Jew of constitutional law." Another academic lawyer complained that *Roe* made a moral question "into a pragmatic issue of ad hoc balancing to be settled by five or more justices. Illustrating again its cleverness and result orientation, the Court reported that constitutional doctrine broke down neatly into trimesters." Judged on the criterion of "intellectual honesty," he concluded, "the Burger Court may have marked the low point in the Supreme Court's not always illustrious history." On grounds of craft, he and others believed, it would make law professors nostalgic for the Warren Court.[85]

That it did. Though *Roe* might have turned out all right substantively, who knew what else the Nixon appointees had up their sleeves? Did they see the record of the Warren Court and *Roe* as license to do whatever they wished? How else to explain their behavior in *Gedulig* v. *Aiello,* when a majority of the Burger Court ruled that discrimination against pregnant women did not constitute a sex-based classification? How else to explain the constant "wavering" of the Burger Court?[86]

In short, since so many law professors continued to believe in the power of courts to effect social change of which they approved, the counter-majoritarian difficulty loomed larger than ever. *Roe* plunged constitutional theory into "epistemological crisis," rekindling interest in judicial review and in the alleged conflict between judicial review and democracy. Legal scholars' task, as they saw it, was to demonstrate that though *Brown* had been correctly decided, *Lochner* and *Roe* had not. It was a worthy mission, one which cast legal scholars as "significant con-stitutional actors" and "minor oracles" whose scholarship was also Su-preme Court advocacy. The effort to come to grips with legal realism, which had spurred process theory, the counter-majoritarian difficulty, and academic reactions to the Burger Court, began anew.[87]

CHAPTER 2

"LAW AND"

This time, law professors looked outward to other disciplines. Economist Paul Samuelson observed that though law schools had long been "an alien and unassimilated element in the body politic of the university," they became part of it "for the first time" in the 1970s. Because of the job crisis among academics, individuals who might once have opted to become humanists or social scientists were choosing to join law faculties. Tenured professors in the humanities and social sciences may have earned more and taught less than they did in previous decades. The young were not so fortunate. Earning a doctorate consumed six to ten years and was followed by exile, if one were lucky, to a series of one-year jobs in obscure schools at starvation wages. "At the 1970 meeting of the American Historical Association there were 2,481 applicants for 188 listed positions, and competition was so fierce that security measures had to be introduced to keep those seeking jobs from destroying invitations to interviews addressed to their competitors." The J.D. demanded only three years. After editing the law review and completing the requisite judicial clerkships, a beginning law professor could earn a great deal more than the humanist or social scientist. In all likelihood, a full professorship would follow in five years.[1]

Unlike departments in the humanities and social sciences, law schools had to tenure new faculty members because in the early 1970s business was booming. Ironically, in the aftermath of Watergate, everyone, so it seemed, wanted to go to law school. Over 135,000 Law School Admission Tests were administered in 1973–74, nearly 14,000 more than the previous year and almost twice as many as those given in any year of the 1960s. The more than 125,000 enrolled law students in 1976 paid more than $275 million in tuition.[2]

Like the realists and scholars in the law and society movement, law professors of the 1970s, some of whom were humanists and social scientists manqués, yearned to incorporate other disciplines in their work. Even those who might never have considered going to graduate school grazed in interdisciplinary pastures. Two of the legal scholars who turned to political philosophy in the 1970s, Frank Michelman and Bruce Ackerman, for instance, were products of what Erwin N. Griswold called "the traditional law school mill." That is, they had the same qualifications as the generation of law professors who preceded them—"high grades in law school—very high." They joined many other academic lawyers in writing of the potential that law possessed to interact with other disciplines.[3]

The appearance of Lawrence Tribe's *American Constitutional Law* in 1978, the first treatise to venture "a unified analysis of constitutional law" since Thomas Cooley's *Constitutional Limitations* more than a century earlier, was the exception that proved the rule. A political liberal, Warren Court devotee, and 1966 graduate of Harvard Law School who would never stop arguing cases before the Supreme Court or writing for judges, Tribe pointed out that all judicial decisions "inescapably" involved "taking sides. . . . Judicial authority to determine when to defer to others in constitutional matters is a procedural form of substantive power; judicial restraint is but another form of judicial activism." He advocated "a more candidly creative role than conventional scholarship has accorded the courts," proceeding "on the premise of a relatively large judicial role" and the idea that "federal courts have a special mission in defending substantive personal interests from governmental action that overreaches because of its unduly limited constituency—action that oppresses people because they are outsiders." Making a structural argument reminiscent of Charles Black's, Tribe rejected "the assumptions characteristic of Justices like Felix Frankfurter and scholars like Alexander Bickel: the highest mission of the Supreme Court, in my view, is not to conserve judicial credibility, but in the Constitution's own phrase, 'to form a more perfect Union' between right and rights within that charter's necessarily evolutionary design." Tribe mocked the "antimajoritarian difficulty" and "the usual hand-wringing over issues of judicial capacity and legitimacy." According to him, "Arguments about the legitimacy of judicial review are ultimately metaconstitutional: the relevant considerations are political, philosophical and historical in the broadest sense." That was exactly the point: in the 1970s, scholars were more interested in the reconciliation of judicial review with democracy than the opinions, or raw materials, of constitutional law, and they were more inclined to think of political, philosophical, and historical considerations.[4]

Yale's Arthur Leff remarked that many law professors of the 1970s spoke in terms of "law and." Contemporaries had ridiculed the legal realists' interdisciplinary ventures, and the empiricism of law and society had only appealed to some. The young legal scholars of the 1970s made it *fashionable* for junior and senior law professors to try interdisciplinary perspectives. Richard Posner declared it "no secret that many law professors have lost interest in the traditional undertakings of legal research."[5]

THE SEARCH FOR OBJECTIVE FOUNDATIONS OF JUSTICE

One group of law professors, who shared Tribe's commitment to a rights-based theory of the Constitution, became enamored of political philosophy. John Rawls enthralled them. His 1971 book, *A Theory of Justice,* won the Coif Award, awarded triennially by the Association of American Law Schools for the best book written on law. Rawls's effort there to develop a rights-based constitutionalism grounded on substantive and objective principles of justice promised a way out of legal realism's subjectivism by integrating constitutional decisionmaking with moral philosophy. At a time when Robert Nozick was about to elegize the "minimal state" in *Anarchy, State, and Utopia,* Rawls promoted political and philosophical liberalism.[6]

Rawls espoused a theory that favored "the right," justice—which was prior to and presumed no concept of "the good." The hypothetical person behind a "veil of ignorance," which left the individual unaware of his or her education, income level, or values and particular vision of "the good," would select this theory of justice, he insisted. Rawls's imaginary individuals chose freely, unaware of personal desires or goals. "They do not know how the various alternatives will affect their own particular case and they are obliged to evaluate principles solely on the basis of general consideration." Rawls maintained they would prefer the right to the subjective good, and would discard a utilitarian theory of justice directed at achieving the greatest good for the greatest number. "Utilitarianism does not take seriously the distinction between persons." Nor would such people argue the ends justified the means. They would opt for "pure procedural justice," or "the Kantian interpretation of justice as fairness."[7]

Here was a theory to which even Earl Warren would have warmed, based as it was on equality and social justice, or, in Rawlsian terms, on maximum individual equality and the "difference principle." That principle provided that "social and economic inequity . . . are just only if they result in compensating benefits for everyone, and in particular for the least advantaged members of society." Yet Rawls gave hope to process theorists by separating law from politics as Kant might have done, though Warren did not. Citing Wechsler's plea for "principled decisions in law," Rawls pledged that his theory of justice would revive the rule of law *and* reconcile the tension between liberty and equality. *"A Theory of Justice* formulates as well as any book to date the principle of justice expressed by the Constitution," one law professor raved.[8]

As part of his continuing effort to bridge constitutional law and theory with political theory and philosophy, Frank Michelman of Harvard briefly yoked Rawls's work to his own. Michelman sought to justify the Court's enforcement of a governmental duty to provide for individuals' "minimum welfare" in order to increase participation in the political process. Unlike his 1960s counterparts, who had less of a need to do so, because the Court appeared headed in that direction, Michelman also used his first *Harvard Law Review* "Foreword" to urge the Court to assume this role.[9]

And during the early years of the Burger Court, it looked as if he might succeed. In fact, it appeared that the Burger Court might even hold wealth a suspect classification, requiring the Court to subject laws harming the poor to strict scrutiny rather than simply to determine whether they were rational, a step the Warren Court had only anticipated in dicta. But when the Supreme Court refused to declare wealth a suspect classification in 1973, some legal liberals became less optimistic. For others, such as Owen Fiss, the Court's 1976 decision in *Washington* v. *Davis,* requiring that those alleging equal protection clause violations in school segregation cases prove intent to segregate, represented Thermidor.[10]

In the mid-1970s, Fiss said later, law professors become estranged from the Supreme Court. And the Court returned their hostility. Chief Justice Burger lambasted the law schools for lawyer incompetence, and flayed the "young people who go into the law primarily on the theory that they can change the world by litigation in the courts." Justice William Rehnquist attacked the notion of "a living constitution" as "a formula for an end run around popular government." Legal scholars' isolation from what had once been their most important audience made them both more similar and more receptive to academics in other fields. The legal academy retained the fantasy of "maintaining a kind of interlocking directorate between itself and the Court." As the judiciary became less appealing, though, law professors were writing less for judges and more for each other.[11]

The shift in scholarship worried some law professors. For one example, "it would be a shame if the lawyer who does philosophy were to be judged solely by other lawyers," Richard Posner said. Who would separate "the experts" from "the charlatans"? Law review editors?[12]

In a sense, Posner was fretting needlessly, for legal scholarship was not changing all that much. Most academic lawyers were still courting judges. Even most of the scholarship of those who now dotted their articles with references to Rawls was traditional and focused on judicial decision making.[13]

Much of the scholarship was directed at awakening the spirit of the Warren Court. It was not always clear the law professors knew the

Warren era had ended, though some legal liberals were partially shifting their attention from the Supreme Court to lower federal courts, and from federal courts to the state courts. Opportunity of a sort struck in 1977, when the Court invalidated a congressional attempt to bring state employees within federal wage-and-hour standards. Many Court-watchers, including Justice Brennan and the other three dissenters, viewed the majority's decision in *National League of Cities* v. *Usery,* as "a step back to the pre–New Deal era in which the Court routinely found reasons to limit the exercise of Congress' commerce power." It should have been apparent to the legal liberals—and it probably was to the pessimists among them—that they now faced the conservative hegemony on the Court they had feared. Their students could see it: the editors of the *Yale Law Journal* dedicated their symposium on *National League of Cities* to Brennan, noting that "we have entered a new era in the history of the Supreme Court and a new jurisprudence is ascendant." Yet in an ironic and stunning symposium article, which tried to seize victory from the jaws of defeat by pointing to the incoherence of the opinion and providing a gloss on it he himself characterized as "perverse," Michelman claimed "to see at work in the Supreme Court's own *NLC* ['*National League of Cities*'] opinion a premise ascribing special service responsibilities to the states."[14]

Meanwhile Bruce Ackerman's success in the early 1970s provided reason for retaining hope in the federal courts. Vigorous enforcement of housing codes would help the indigent, Ackerman argued. It would not hurt them by increasing rents and reducing the housing supply. Washington, D.C., Circuit Court of Appeals Judge Skelly Wright cited Ackerman's article in his important 1972 decision establishing an implied warranty of habitability. Ackerman's work, Wright said, supported the proposition that "[w]hen code enforcement is seriously pursued, market forces generally prevent landlords from passing on their increased costs through rent increases."[15]

Traditionally, citation by an important court represented a high point for the legal scholar. As one schooled in the realist tradition, however, Ackerman may have wondered how much his work really influenced Wright. Did the citation constitute window dressing? For whatever reason—perhaps growing doubt about the value of doctrinal work, perhaps interdisciplinary currents—Ackerman, like Michelman, was broadening the way he wrote about law.

And Ackerman too was a Rawls enthusiast. In *Social Justice in the Liberal State,* a book that constituted a long, friendly debate with Rawls and included a modified original position, Ackerman attacked "the conflict between self-fulfillment and social justice" by producing a theory of justice based on dialogue and neutral conversations between individuals on how best to share resources. "The hard truth is this: There is no moral meaning hidden in the bowels of the universe," Ackerman claimed. That was no reason to despair. "We may create our own meanings, you and I." Miraculously, neither that process nor accepting liberalism would involve "Big Questions of a highly controversial character." Along with Rawls, Ackerman helped to "popularize the notion that something called Neutrality was at the heart of contemporary liberalism. . . . [A] principle purpose of my book about *The Liberal State* is to convince you that a commitment to Neutrality leads neither to intellectual bankruptcy nor empty formalism, but to an incisive form of liberal political culture."[16]

Still another Rawls convert, Ronald Dworkin, articulated a rights-based jurisprudence designed to constrain judicial discretion, rationalize the Warren Court's record, integrate law with morals, and promote democracy. Where Bickel linked democracy to majority will, Dworkin thought in terms of rights against the majority. For Dworkin, the debate about the propriety of the Warren Court's imposition of its values on the nation obscured "the issue of what moral rights an individual has against the state." Giving the Warren Court a "rights" spin, he announced that rights were "trumps." Dworkin's idealized judge, whom he named Hercules, possessed a particular vision of rights foundationalism, which treated equality as more important than liberty. Hercules believed that the duty of government was to treat people "with equal concern and respect," and that judicial decisions must "enforce existing political rights." As Dworkin put it in *Taking Rights Seriously:*

> Constitutional law can make no genuine advance until it isolates
> the problem of rights against the state and makes that problem
> part of its own agenda. That argues for a fusion of constitutional
> law and moral theory, a connection that, incredibly, has yet to